Alabama Ghosts

they are among us

Holly Smith

SWEETW
PRES.

Table of Contents

They Are Among Us

They Are Among Us

I don't believe in free lunches. I don't believe the check is in the mail. I don't believe in coincidences. But I have to confess, it's true that occasionally someone does buy me lunch. And sometimes, the check really is in the mail. And I suppose you could say that, depending on your perspective, coincidences that are difficult to explain any other way just do happen at least once or twice to everyone. So I guess when I say that I don't believe in ghosts, I have to also say that I'm willing to make exceptions.

Growing up in Alabama, I was always fascinated by the variety of ghost stories that abound in this state. They have been part of my family's heritage. My great-great-great grandmother told them to my great-grandmother, who told them to my father, who in turn shared them with me. My older brother and his friends always tried to frighten me with their spooky stories, as did the pastor of my church, a high school English teacher, and other friends. So I guess you can say I've heard ghost stories all of my life from all types of people. I can't say I have ever actually seen one, in the sense of something white and wispy floating through the air. But I have had experiences that are impossible to explain in the sense of the rational, material world.

Unexplained breezes have sometimes brushed my face in a closed room. Small items like toothbrushes and shoes have mysteriously been moved, when no one was home, from one part of the house to another. Lights have turned on and off by themselves. Doors untouched by human hands have slammed out of the blue. And I'm quite sure that, one time when I was lost in the dark, I distinctly heard a voice telling me which direction to go. I'm not saying that there definitely are ghosts—just that there are things we don't know how to explain.

I've kind of made it an unofficial hobby to collect ghost stories from people I know. I was thrilled at the opportunity to put some of them down in this book. I like to think that, in having their stories collected in print, some of these ghosts might find some kind of peace or at least a certain satisfaction they have been looking for. The story of David Hanby has always fascinated me, for example. Shot in the back by Union soldiers while out looking for his cattle near Pinson. I think of him, wandering forever, looking for those cattle. Or the ghosts that swirl around the Mighty Wurlitzer in Birmingham's Alabama Theatre. I always thought that place was a bit creepy! Or the mysterious fisherman of Lake Tohlocco. He takes your fishing rod, then just as mysteriously, returns it.

Maybe in sharing these stories with readers like you, I will be doing my little part in helping preserve these tales as well as bringing new ones to light. You might even have some of your own. After all, whether you believe or not, you have to admit you can't always explain everything, especially if it happens in the deepest, darkest part of the night.

One more thing: many of the names in these stories have been changed—to protect the haunted. You know who you are.

Holly Smith

Old Man Matthews

Old Man Matthews

James, Timothy, Scott, Chloe, and Michelle were playing cards on a porch in Evergreen one hot, steamy summer evening. As the sun went down, a soft breeze began to blow. Slowly, the sun disappeared behind the trees. A light rain began to fall. The moon and stars were hidden by a band of clouds.

"Tonight is the perfect night to tell ghost stories," Scott said.

"Ooh, ghost stories," replied James. "That sounds like fun."

As the children began to exchange tales, Michelle spoke up. "Stories are for sissies. Let's try to find some real ghosts."

"How do you expect us to do that?" asked Timothy.

"By exploring a cemetery."

"*What*?!?" Chloe shrieked.

"We'll walk through an old cemetery," Michelle repeated. "McConnio is just over that hill. We'll walk around in it, and maybe we'll get lucky and see something."

"Quit talking big, Michelle. You're too chicken to walk through a cemetery at night," Scott jabbed.

"I will, too. You're the one that's afraid," Michelle rebutted.

"I bet you won't either," James retorted.

"I'll take that bet. In fact, I bet you five dollars that I'll walk to a grave in the very center of it by myself."

"Well, if you go by yourself, how will we know you actually made it?" Scott remarked.

"I'll leave something on the grave."

"What will you leave?"

"I don't know."

James had an idea. "What about a fork? When you get to the grave, stick a fork in it. Then we can all go back in the morning, and if the fork is there, you win the bet."

"Deal."

"What a minute. A fork? Why a fork? That's like the most random thing I've ever heard," Scott questioned.

"Because we don't know what may already be there. What are the odds that there will already be a fork in the grave."

"Oh, okay. Deal."

Timothy had been very quiet. He knew what lay just over the hill. In the center of that cemetery stood the grave of an old Confederate soldier, known only as Old Man Matthews. Timothy had heard stories of people seeing his ghost on rainy nights. He chimed in, "I don't think you should do it, Michelle."

"Why not?"

"I just don't think you should."

"Unless you give me a good reason not to, I'm going in, and your reason better not be that I'll see a ghost— that's why I'm going."

Timothy silently stared at his shoes.

Noting his reaction, Scott said, "I'm raising the bet. I'll give you ten dollars to stick a fork in Old Man Matthews's grave."

"I second that," James piped in.

"I still don't think you should do it."

"I agree with Timothy," Chloe said worriedly.

"I'm not afraid of anything," Michelle stated confidently. "Let's go."

"Who's in?" Scott asked.

"I am."

"I guess I am too."

"I'm certainly not staying here by myself," Chloe replied.

The five children made their way over the hill to the edge of the cemetery.

"How will you know which one is his grave?"

"It's the only one with a headless statue, just on the other side of the hill," Timothy pronounced.

"Okay, give me the flashlight," Michelle asserted as she walked alone into the graveyard.

"Be careful!" Chloe called out as Michelle disappeared over the hill. "Why do I get the feeling that's the last time I'll see her?"

"Oh, quit acting like a scared little kid," Scott said harshly. "She won't make it to the grave. She'll be back before you know it."

As the four children waited for Michelle to return, Timothy told the others of Old Man Matthews. After serving in the Civil War, he returned home but was a very changed man. He always talked to himself and hardly spoke to anyone else. One of his best friends was killed in the war, and Matthews used to visit his grave at McConnio every week. One particularly steamy July evening, Matthews ran frantically into town yelling, "The Yankees are here! The Yankees are here!" No one in town knew what he was talking about—the war had been over for five years.

Matthews eventually confided in a neighbor, saying he had seen Union soldiers roaming through the cemetery. He never forgot that evening and spoke of it for years, even up until the night he died. He always said he wanted to be buried near his friend, so he could keep an eye on him and protect him from the Union soldiers who were trying to destroy his hometown.

"And that's why I didn't want her to go in there. I was afraid Old Man Matthews might think she was a Union soldier trying to destroy his beloved Evergreen," Timothy summed up.

"I wish you had spoken up sooner."

"Relax, she'll be back soon," Scott chimed in.

But the four children waited and waited and waited. After an hour there was still no sign of Michelle. The sound of thunder rumbled in the distance. They began to worry.

"See, I told you she shouldn't have gone."

"Yeah I'm starting to agree with Chloe. She's been gone an awful long time," James interjected.

"I think she could have been there and back several times by now," Timothy uttered.

"You guys are bigger sissies than Chloe. Michelle's just playing a trick on us. She's trying to scare us," Scott asserted.

Another hour passed; there was still no sign of Michelle, and the storm was getting closer.

"Maybe we should go for help."

"Yeah let's go, Scott."

"Okay, let's go."

The four frightened children ran to find help.

Meanwhile, Michelle was having a hard time finding the headless-statue grave marker. She paused and stared at the sky. Every second it grew darker and the storm would be there soon. Finally, she saw the statue.

Shaking, she slowly bent down to stick the fork in the grave. Still standing over it, she suddenly felt something cold and wet wrap around her ankle. She gasped. The only sound was the thud of a flashlight hitting the ground.

An hour later the other four children returned with the sheriff. "It should be over there," Timothy reported, pointing and squinting in the darkness. The group made its way to the grave and found Michelle lying on the ground.

"Michelle! Michelle! Are you okay?" Scott tried to wake her up.

Slowly, Michelle opened her eyes. "Scott, is that you?" she asked groggily.

"Yes, what happened? We were so worried."

"I don't know. I felt something around my ankle and got scared."

"I think you fainted." Scott looked down to see that Michelle's foot was tangled up in some ivy. She had then stuck the fork in it, holding the ivy down so she couldn't move her foot.

David the Ghost

David the Ghost

The city of Mobile has many beautiful old homes gracing the oak-lined streets of the Oakleigh Garden historic district. Several of them are large antebellum beauties, with towering columns and old slave-made bricks. Others are from the Victorian era, beautifully restored, covered in decorative intricate cutwork and painted in the almost garish colors of the age. Still others have the simple elegant influences of the Arts and Crafts style from the early 1900s.

The house that Elizabeth Harris spent her childhood in was from this time period. The home had a very open and airy quality to it. The living room and dining room both had fourteen-foot ceilings, and the windows were almost to the floor and bathed the hardwood floors with sunlight throughout the year. Four tapered columns elegantly and simply separated the living room and the dining room. All the bedrooms had twelve-foot ceilings and those tall wonderful windows. The plaster work walls were in nearly perfect condition and were a lovely contrast to the simple and exquisitely detailed woodwork, which was all a golden tiger oak.

Elizabeth had moved to the historic house when she

was only six, with her mother, Beth; her father, William; and her younger brother, Drew. During her childhood, she had played all around the house and grounds, content to entertain herself with her toys and her cat, Tigger.

Perhaps it was Tigger who first noticed something was not quite right. Beth began to notice Tigger intently staring at nothing. Then, without warning, he would bristle, all of his fur standing on end, and then run at full gallop out of the room. She mentioned to Will that Tigger had been acting strangely. However, they had both thought it was funny, though it was a bit creepy to watch.

One sunny winter afternoon, as Beth walked past, Tigger shot out of Elizabeth's room as if a pack of rabid coon hounds was after him. Elizabeth was sitting in her room laughing out loud and serving tea to an imaginary friend. "How sweet," Beth said to herself as she watched unnoticed from the doorway.

By spring, both Beth and Will saw a change in little Elizabeth. She had always been an imaginative child, but she was spending more and more time with her invisible pal, who now had a name: David.

Not only that, but everyone in the household had noticed odd items like hairbrushes, books, and small toys missing from their rooms. When Elizabeth was asked if she had seen or taken these items, she just giggled and said, "Oh, I bet David got it!" Then she yelled, "David, put Mom's hairbrush back!" She put her little hand to her face and whispered, "He usually puts it the last place you looked for it." And then off she was again playing.

Will and Beth were becoming a bit alarmed—not as alarmed as Tigger the cat, who growled as he ran past Elizabeth's room. More and more strange things began to happen. The missing items that at first had been only monthly happenings were becoming daily occurrences. This was unnerving at best.

Then, their son, Drew, woke up one morning with the window open, moss and mud over the floor of his bedroom. Strangely, there were no footprints outside in the red clay below his window.

Finally, Will and Beth had had enough! They decided to challenge this "David" fellow. They stood in the living room next to a large ten-foot tall bookcase that stretched the length of one wall and said, "If there is a spirit here, prove it!"

They waited holding their breath and each other's hands. A few very tense moments passed, and then, out of the corner of his eye, Will saw a book on the very top shelf begin to slide out very, very slowly. He found himself unable to speak and nudged Beth to look. They stared in silent disbelief as the book slid out, hovered for a minute, and then dropped to the floor with a tremendous thud! Both husband and wife were terrified and stood dumbstruck for quite a while. Will broke the silence with, "Okay, you are here. I want you to quit playing with my little girl, and stop all of this nonsense right *now*, or I'm calling a priest!"

Days and then weeks went by, and there were no signs of the trickster. Things stayed where they were put, and the cat settled down. Elizabeth would mention from time to time missing her friend, but that passed also with time.

The months rolled into years, and the invisible friend was forgotten until one evening. Drew and Elizabeth were teenagers, and it wasn't unusual for any number of their friends to come over unannounced and hang out for an evening of MTV or videos. Beth and Will were on their way to the den to commandeer the TV remote from the teens, when a young man wearing dark gray with dark hair ran from Elizabeth's door and into Drew's.

"Hey, don't run in the house!" bellowed Will, and the parents shrugged.

"Teenagers!" Beth murmured. They laughed and talked about how they never should have gotten MTV. Will opened the door to the den and was instantly overwhelmed by the loud obnoxious music of the eighties. "Turn it down! And by the way, tell your friends to stop running in the house. One of them almost ran us over on his way to your room. Who was that kid anyway?"

Drew and Elizabeth looked blankly at their parents. "Um, there's nobody here, Dad. It's just us really."

"Well, who ran past us?" asked Beth.

"I don't know. We were here the whole time."

Everyone flooded out of the den and searched the house, and just as the children had said, they were the only ones there. Beth and Will could feel the hair standing up on the backs of their necks when Elizabeth giggled and said, "You know, it was probably David."

"Yeah," said Drew. "Have you guys never seen him before?"

The Harris family decided to move not too long after that night. It wasn't that David was a malevolent spirit. He wasn't—he was just a bit of a prankster. They never could find any information about the history of the house in the Oakleigh Garden district, even though they searched Mobile's archives. Who David was, when he died, or why he haunted the lovely home remained a mystery for decades.

Years later, one Halloween, Elizabeth and her children—five-year-old daughter, Nicole; six-year-old son, Alex; and eight-year-old son, Ryan—were trick-ortreating in her old neighborhood. On a balmy fall evening, they walked up the same sidewalk and steps she used to hopscotch on seemingly eons before. Alex rang the bell, and all three sang out, "Trick or treat!" as the nice old man opened the door.

In the South, you never meet a stranger, and the usual chit-chat about costumes and pumpkins meandered on until Alex pulled on the man's sleeve and announced rather loudly, "Mommy used to live in this house when she was my age!"

"Really," the man said slowly. He chose this moment to introduce himself as David Forrest Taylor, a seventy-year-old retired businessman. He had traveled the world for his business and decided in his dotage to return to the hometown of his birth. "You can call me Dave if you like. By the way, you may think I am a little crazy for asking, but did anything strange ever happen to you here?"

Elizabeth smiled. "Oh, yes, the house *is* haunted, but not by anything evil or malevolent. He is just more of a prankster and likes to play tricks—nothing serious though. He actually was my invisible friend when I was little. Coincidentally, I always called him David. How funny that you two not only share the house now but share names, too!" Elizabeth was laughing about this until she noticed all the color had drained from her new friend.

"David!" he gasped! "How did you know his name was David!?"

"Um, that's just what I always called him. The whole family called him by David. Are you okay? You look a little pale. Can I help you sit down?"

"Yes, thank you. I think I could really use a chair right now."

Yet again Elizabeth found herself crossing the threshold of her old home. She helped Dave into one of his comfortable leather club chairs and covered him with a soft chenille throw from an adjacent chair. The children made themselves at home as children often do, browsing the living room as if it were a museum—and in many ways it was. Dave must have been very well traveled indeed. There were artifacts from every part of the globe scattered around the room. African masks, weapons from the Amazon, Greek pottery, and all matter of unusual objects d'art were everywhere.

The color began to return to Dave's face, and he smiled and gave descriptions to the children when they would ask, "What's this, and that, and that?" It soon became obvious that he had recovered from his shock.

"Dave, I don't mean to be nosy, but I can't help but be terribly curious about your reaction to what I said outside," Elizabeth said, lightly patting the old man's hand.

"Ah, of course!" he said. "You see, I bought this house because it was built by my great-grandparents Forrest and Annabelle Taylor. They had two children, Ashton and David, for whom I am named. Ashton was my grandfather, and he was eight when the house was built in 1906. David was only six when they moved in. Apparently, they were all very happy here until 1912, when David came down with polio and sadly died.

"My great-grandparents were crushed by the loss of their little boy and couldn't bear living in a house with such sorrow. My grandfather used to drive me past this house as a child and tell me stories about his long lost little brother. It doesn't surprise me that David the ghost is a trickster. He was quite a handful when he was a little boy! He used to hide things and chase the cat all about the house. By all accounts, he was a very playful and happy little boy."

"I had noticed a few strange occurrences when I moved. However, I just thought it was a memory lapse due to my old age," Dave said, grinning. "I guess I was surprised that he had made himself that well known to you and your family. It just shocked me that you knew his name."

"I'm glad that I could give you a good fright on Halloween!" said Elizabeth. She and the children all giggled at that. "It's still early yet, and I think my little monsters need to extort more candy from the neighbors! It has been an absolute pleasure meeting you and finally knowing the answer to our little mystery. Thank you so much for telling us your story."

Dave stood up and walked them toward the door. "Well, I feel much better now. And I like that I am roommates with my great-uncle David! Not every body can say that! Y'all please feel free to come by and visit anytime!"

As Dave began to close the massive oak front door, Elizabeth turned and waved goodnight to him. As she did, just for a second, over his shoulder she saw a faint shadow.

"Good night, David. It's really good to see you again," she whispered. The door closed, and the happy bunch romped down the sidewalk and back out into the night, searching for yet another doorbell to ring.

The Brown Family

The Brown Family

The sun lowered itself in west Alabama, and Jonathan Brown watched it settle behind the trees at the end of his field. He unhitched his horse from the plow, heading toward home and the meal Sarah was sure to be placing on the table. Johnny and Rachel would be playing as they brought fresh water from the well. Jonathan smiled to himself and plodded through the low-growing trees.

The sky was quickly fading to a swallowing blackness, and Jonathan thought he could smell a storm on the horizon. He paused to wipe the sweat from his forehead. "Nothing worse than Alabama humidity in the summer," he spoke aloud. Suddenly remembering he was alone, Jonathan walked a little quicker. As he passed the familiar hollowed-out ash tree and came into sight of his front gate, he stopped and stared.

The wooden fence lay splintered and lopsided on the ground. His eyes slowly moved from the broken slats to the top of his house rising over the crest of the hill. He walked further, wondering what had happened, hoping Johnny had simply been overzealous in his chores. More of the house came into view; the upstairs windows were dark and silent.

"Wonder where everybody is," he mumbled, his deep southern accent drawing out each word. Jonathan took a few more steps before pausing longer to survey the yard. Grass and shrubs were uprooted and strewn about the walkway as if something large had moved quickly and harshly through the yard. The bark of the lone oak tree was stripped and discarded around the roots. As he walked under the tree he could feel the raindrops start to hit his hat and shoulders.

As he stood under the oak tree he heard drops hitting him and the ground. He felt the wind rush about his feet and throw dust into the air. Jonathan started up the path leading to his home's porch and nearly tripped on a tin bucket lying on the ground. His eyes strained as they looked toward the front door and saw it had been smashed inward. Jonathan's heart started beating faster and a foreboding sense of dread settled on his mind. Panic seemed to grip his body as he slowly climbed the creaky porch and stepped into the dark house. The wind suddenly blew harder, slamming the already opened front door. Jonathan jumped.

The house screamed silence. All he could hear were the rubber soles of his boots scraping across the hardwood floors as he tentatively walked into the house. Normally the hallways were filled with light and laughter, but this evening every corner oozed blackness

31

and despair. He glanced to the right—towards the kitchen. Tonight there were no smells emanating from the small space—only emptiness.

Jonathan began to tremble. He paused, trying to remember where his family might be. He picked up a fallen lantern from the hallway table. Striking a match, he lit the tiny candle and raised the rusty metal shutter, sending a small beam racing across the room. The tiny flame was a bright beacon in the darkness.

A raspy breath escaped from his lungs as Jonathan saw the walls of his home. Whatever it was that had passed through there had left a trail of broken furniture and the remains of Sarah's dinner through the house that Jonathan could only follow. His heart pounded within his chest, beating louder, making his ears ache.

The path continued up the stairs. Jonathan eased up them; the lantern made eerie shadows on the walls, sending chills down his spine. Long, deep scratches scored the floor leading to each of the bedrooms. As he passed the washroom, the faint drip from the leaky faucet in the bathroom echoed throughout the hall. His heavy breathing matched the beat of the dripping water.

He reached the nursery where his son Abram should be sleeping. He walked to the crib and peered inside hoping to find his son, but instead a broken rattle and a slashed corn doll lay in his place. Seeing the mangled toys was more than he could take. He felt the color drain from his face.

Overcome with emotion, Jonathan sprinted down the stairs and outside, his ears roaring loudly. Calling for his wife and children, he ran around the yard like a maniac. Unable to find anything, he dropped to his knees under the lone oak tree in desperation. His heart felt as if it might explode.

The rain was falling heavily in large droplets that ran through the grit and sweat on Jonathan's neck and soaked his now hatless head. Larger, darker drops were falling now, soaking his clothing. Looking down, he saw his arm was covered with what appeared to be blood. Glancing at the tree above him, he found what he had been searching for—what he had feared. His mouth opened and a noiseless scream emitted from deep within his stomach. He continued to stare up into the many branches of the oak tree.

Some say if you drive a few hours southwest from Montgomery through small towns on narrow winding country roads you come to a little place called Jackson, Alabama. If you take this trip on a windy day in the late summer, you come to a secluded farmhouse set back from the road. It is a modest place with a large ash tree by a broken wood slat fence. A lone oak tree stands in the yard. An overgrown path leads to a deserted old house.

Most of the porch is now overrun with kudzu, making it impossible to get a closer look, but if you wait until late at night, a silent dark figure appears. It moves about the yard, making its way toward the house as if looking for something. It disappears into the bleak house, only to return minutes later. The form can be seen frantically searching the house and the yard. Suddenly, the figure will drop to the ground, almost out of sight. It kneels at the base of the oak tree, and if you watch closely, you can almost see his mouth moving. Jonathan Brown is screaming for his family. And if the moon is positioned just right, in the top of the oak tree, four bodies can be seen slowly dripping their lives onto the ground.

The Haunting of
Ashville

The Haunting of Ashville

The first settlers of Ashville arrived in the area around 1817. St. Clair County was then established in November 1818, making it older than the state of Alabama. Ashville was first founded as St. Clairsville. The name was later changed to Ashville in honor of John Ash, who played a vital role in establishing the town. Chosen as the county seat because its location in the center of the county, Ashville was incorporated in 1822. Given its age and history, it is not surprising that Ashville has a haunted past.

The Indian Drums

General Andrew Jackson came down from Tennessee before Alabama became a state. It was around 1813, and there were no white families living in the Coosa River area yet. Only hunters and traders seemed to be brave enough to scope out the land surrounding Indian villages. General Jackson and three thousand men entered the area and made their headquarters at Ten Islands of the Coosa River, also known as Fort Strother.

Jackson sent groups of men out to search for

supplies, giving the men orders to destroy any Indian villages they encountered. It was mid-October when Colonel Dyer discovered he was camped within five miles of Chief Cataula's village on Big Canoe Creek. At the same time, Cataula's men found out about the troops. They knew their village would be in danger of being destroyed and themselves most likely killed in the process. They realized they needed the help of another Indian tribe eight miles away. Late that night they pounded on their war drums, calling for help. The loud, resonate ker-boom, ker-boom, ker-boom of the drums pierced the dark silence of the moonless night.

The sound of the drums reached the ears of Colonel Dyer, who immediately knew what was happening. An attack was inevitable, and Dyer thought it best to strike first rather than be ambushed. He and his men made their way to the village.

The Indians held their own but were greatly outnumbered. Dyer burned the village and took twenty-nine Creek prisoners, a herd of cattle, and some other food supplies back to Fort Strother and General Jackson.

The only Creeks killed in the attack were two of Chief Cataula's sons. To this day, on cold, moonless nights, the ker-boom of their drums can be heard echoing in the darkness.

Old Tawassee

General Jackson removed most of the Creek Indians from the area, but a few were still around. They lived in a place near Dean's Spring called Tawassee, which meant "sanctuary" or "safe place."

By 1829, most of theses Indians were gone, but one, a thieving villain, had managed to stay behind. The Indians had been causing problems up and down the river valley. They loved to break into houses and barns, stealing whatever food items they could get their hands on. No one's property was safe.

After being caught carrying two slabs of bacon from Mr. Jones's smokehouse, this particular Indian was whipped and released. Only known as Old Tawassee, the pilferer returned a few days later. Mrs. Jones was out back boiling and beating laundry. Seeking revenge for his thrashing, he snuck onto the Jones's farmland. Only days before he had been warned never to return. He grabbed a stick and knocked Mrs. Jones in the head. She slumped to the ground, unconscious.

As in every small town, news traveled fast. The only Indian left in town, Old Tawassee had no place to hide. The sheriff, Colonel John Massey, wouldn't stand for that type of behavior. Tawassee was soon apprehended, and before he could utter a word in his defense, he was standing under a gigantic oak tree in the town square.

A crowd quickly gathered to see the first hanging in the area. Whispering with curiosity, they watched the Indian intently.

His neck itching from the raw rope, Tawassee glanced down at the wagon beneath him. He blinked. The rickety wagon jerked out from under him. He tried to stretch and wriggle out of the death trap but was suddenly motionless. His lifeless body began to sway in the soft April breeze.

The townspeople simply stared at him. Not knowing what to do with the corpse, they left him there, swinging.

He hung there for days, gently swinging in the wind.

Finally, Dr. Brewster said he would dispose of the Indian. He and his apprentice cut down the body. Together they stuffed him in a box and carried it to Canoe Creek. They lowered the makeshift coffin into the river, secured it, and promised to return in a few months.

Meanwhile, the river rapids rushed across the body, removing the rough flesh, leaving only Tawassee's bones.

After the winter, Dr. Brewster and his associate returned to retrieve what remained of Old Tawassee. Upon opening the box, they found exactly what they had hoped for—nothing but the bones.

After tediously wiring the bones together, Dr.

Brewster hung the skeleton in a closet in his office, just down from the town square. Many students learned human anatomy from Tawassee's remains that were used as a teaching aid.

The one-year anniversary of the hanging was fast approaching. The first to be hanged from the large oak in the square, Old Tawassee hadn't been forgotten. The tree had quickly become known as the hanging tree.

The morning of that day was eerily calm for an Alabama spring. No winds blew; no clouds were in the sky. The air was the perfect temperature with no humidity. People were milling about on the street, on their way to and from the market that was always set up that time of year. Suddenly, leaves from the hanging tree burst into the air, as the tree began to shake violently. On a closer look, only the limb from which Tawassee was hanged trembled. Frightened, the townspeople scattered. Since most of them lived several miles from town, the people crammed into the few businesses. Every door was locked and every window shut.

The tree stopped shaking, and the leaves landed softly on the ground. As townspeople began moving about, word spread that it had to be Tawassee's ghost. Spreading like wildfire, the news eventually reached Dr. Brewster. "The ghost of Tawassee has returned for his

bones," he heard from several different patients.
Laughing at the ignorance of his fellow man, Dr.
Brewster ignored the accounts.

But that evening, as he and his assistant, Thomas,
were cleaning up to leave the small office, strange sounds
echoed through the silent space. Thomas began to
tremble. He backed into a corner, crouched, and
mumbled, "He's come back to get us!" The sounds
continued for several minutes. Dr. Brewster decided they
were coming from the closet. Slowly opening the creaky
door, he was shocked to find the skeleton of Old
Tawassee shaking violently in the dark.

The Courthouse Ghost

As one of two county seats in St. Clair County (a
branch moved to Pell City in 1902), the courthouse has
always played a vital role in Ashville's history. Court
week was held regularly in the spring and again in the
fall. The "week" would often turn into three or four
weeks, and each time, all the boarding houses in Ashville
would be filled with judges, lawyers, and court reporters.

The courthouse was built before the Civil War in
1844 by Littleton Yarbrough, who had his slave make the
bricks right on the town square. A man by the name of
Jefferson Campbell was hired to lay the bricks. Campbell
had the help of an Irish man with a funny limp. The

Irishman was known as one of the best brick layers in the state, but he would only work on one condition. He had to have his little brown jug with him as he worked.

Each morning the Irishman would fill his jug with moonshine from Mr. Yarbrough's still. He could make one jug last an entire day. When he wasn't drinking from it, he would slide the jug down the wall as he worked.

The Saturday the men were laying the west wall of the building, the Irishman's wife came down to the site, asking to speak with her husband. He obeyed, scurried down the wall, and limped to meet her, leaving his precious jug where he had been working. Campbell wanted to have the wall finished before dark and grew impatient waiting for his helper to return. He continued to work and finished the wall quickly.

The Irishman returned to find the day's work completed and his little brown jug missing. He searched everywhere but couldn't find it. He finally asked Campbell if he had seen it, but he merely shrugged his shoulders. The only answer the Irishman could come up with was that the jug had been bricked into the wall. He panicked and began tapping furiously on the newly bricked wall. He tapped all the way up and down it, listening for any clue that might show the jug's location. The rest of the crew had gone home for long ago, but the little Irishman continued to tap into the night.

He apparently never found his brown jug because on cold windy nights, lone courthouse visitors can still hear his tap-tap-tap on the bricks of the west wall of the building.

The Ashville Museum & Archives

The Ashville Museum & Archives is located within the historic St. Clair County Courthouse. It contains county records, including wills, deeds, births, and deaths, dating back to 1819. The Census of Confederate Soldiers from 1907 and newspapers from as early as 1879 can also be found there.

One woman was instrumental in gathering and organizing all of the genealogical information found in the Archives—Mattie Lou Teague Crow. The author and editor of several books detailing St. Clair County's history, Mrs. Crow grew up in Ashville and spent much of her life researching and tracing her ancestry. A beautiful white-haired woman with a sweet disposition, she expended vast amounts of energy into the archives. It was definitely one of Mrs. Crow's greatest passions. She died at the age of 96 and is buried in the Ashville Cemetery.

Mrs. Crow loved the museum so much that she still visits it on occasion. The information contained in the museum is used by many students conducting research for reports. Jokingly, the current archivist will warn them that they better get their history correct or Mrs. Crow will come after them. One young girl, after concluding her research, told the archivist that she felt something cold brush against her arm while she was searching for information. She said that Mrs. Crow must have been trying to help her find what she needed.

There have been several other reports of visitors seeing a white-haired lady walking around the museum. Ironically, these accounts would have fascinated Mrs. Crow, who grew up hearing ghost stories from her grandmother and in turn shared them with her children, grandchildren, and great-grandchildren.

The Villages

The Villages

It was a dark and stormy night—well, it should have been. It was actually a balmy Alabama evening. A diaphanous haze thick with the acridly sweet scent of mimosas blanketed the darkness where three teenagers drove aimlessly.

Like most teenagers, these three were looking for something that at least slightly resembled entertainment. Sheffield was a very small town to them, and in their words "there wasn't *anything* to do." Unlike many of their contemporaries, these three weren't "into" drinking or drugs or "other things." They were fairly well behaved—for teenagers, anyway.

The leader of the little group was the oldest. Arti was a handsome, tall, dark-headed guy with bright blue-green eyes that tended to have a mischievous twinkle. At sixteen, not only was Arti the instigator of most of the friends' excursions and adventures, he was also the driver.

Robert, at fifteen and a half, was the next eldest. He was smaller in stature than Arti. He had soft brown hair and deep brown eyes that were very expressive against his pale skin. Robert had begun to date Maggie, who was just a little younger at only fifteen. Both boys gave her a great deal of grief about being the baby of the bunch. Maggie had shoulder length red hair, green eyes, and alabaster skin with a smattering of freckles across her nose and cheeks.

Robert had met Maggie at the mall—it being "the *only* place to go" in town. Dating then and dating now are very different things. Dating then meant meeting somewhere and hanging out with your friends, and then maybe stealing a kiss when you dropped your date off at her door. Your date had to be accepted by your friends back then. Arti was Robert's best friend and had been since the first grade. It was very important that Arti like Maggie, and he did, to Robert's relief.

On this particular night, Arti was at the wheel and up for adventure. They had already gone by their ordinary haunts and had become bored with them.

"Where can we go tonight? There's nothing going on!" Robert whined from the passenger seat.

The three bounced ideas around for several minutes before Arti excitedly said, "I know! I know! Let's go to the old abandoned house in the Villages!"

"Cool!" was the response from the other two.

The old abandoned house was built before World War II in a small quaint neighborhood of stuccoed houses with tiled roofs known as the Villages. The

Villages had originally been built on the other side of the Tennessee River in Florence for the workers constructing Wilson Dam, which began in 1918. These homes were moved to Sheffield sometime shortly before the dam was completed, between 1924 and 1927. The original use of the building was thought by the teenagers to be an army barrack, a school, and lastly an apartment building. Whatever it was to begin with, it was abandoned at the moment and was a perfect candidate for exploration and adventure.

Arti turned into the slumbering neighborhood and headed for the darkened target. The house dominated the street. Unlike the other petite bungalows of the Villages, this structure was four stories tall. It loomed an inky silhouette against the azure evening sky. All three friends felt a little foreboding feeling as they passed the expansive façade and cruised around to the back of the hulking abandoned shell of a building.

Arti had done some exploring there earlier in the day and discovered a way in. He had placed a nail against the doorframe, so he could tell if anyone else had gone into his newest conquest. All the other doors had been secured, as well as the multiple sets of windows throughout the home. Arti was first to the door; nope, the nail was still in place! "Looks like we have it all to ourselves!" he said happily.

Robert and Maggie tumbled out of Arti's car and looked up, awestruck. It was truly a massive place. Arti opened the door, and the three ventured into a great room that spanned about twenty-five feet wide by forty feet in length. Along one side of the "great hall," as they called it, were six sets of French doors. It was a beautiful space. There were fireplaces at both ends of the room, and again, two sets of French doors to the stairwells on either end.

Arti had found an old telephone line spool to use as a table and several wooden crates for seats, which was where he chose to put the boom box and flashlights and Cokes and candles and chips and any other thing he thought to bring that might increase their sense of creature comforts. They took their time exploring the vast ballroom-like space. They lit candles on the fireplaces and on the spool, where they also put a large flashlight pointed at the ceiling to bounce light all around, dissipating much of the darkness and giving the great hall almost a cozy feel.

"Let's see the rest of the place," said Robert. And they were off. The three bounded noisily up the stairs and through the many empty and dilapidated rooms. The stairwells were wide with large beautiful arched windows at every landing. Many of the walls between the rooms had been torn out, most likely in preparation for renovation. For the teenagers, it meant they could see from one side of the house to the other on every floor.

The three friends scampered about, playing hide-and-seek and wild games of tag until they decided perhaps they were getting much too loud, and Arti pointed out, "You know, breaking and entering is like a crime, okay."

Maggie suggested going back down to the great room. It was her favorite, and it was also closest to the car if they needed to get out quickly. No one wanted the police, or more importantly, their parents involved. They sat down at the spool table and gleefully snacked, gossiped about high school dramas, and listened to the Cure, Billy Idol, and Boy George.

Arti was in the midst of laughing about what exactly Boy George was when Maggie grabbed his arm and said, "Did you hear that?"

"Hear what?" both boys replied.

"I don't know. It sounded like footsteps over there in the stairwell."

Before Arti could turn off the boom box, the battery-powered flashlight on the table flickered and went out. The music also stopped suddenly, as if all the batteries had drained in a matter of seconds.

"Um, that's kinda creepy," Robert whispered, as he snuggled closer to Maggie, who was listening intently to whatever it was she heard.

"Did it just get colder in here?" Arti was now also whispering.

"Yea, I'm freezing. Maybe we should leave now?" Maggie murmured to Arti.

He was beginning to feel really uneasy and started to gather up everything he had so carefully laid out for the evening's entertainment. Little did he know the real entertainment was about to arrive.

At that moment, the French doors to the far stairwell flew open, and a cold breeze rushed in past the friends, blowing out the candles. Robert grabbed his lighter and relit his candle instantly. "Ol' quick draw!"

"Sshh! Listen!" Maggie was standing up with the boom box in her hands and starting to edge toward the exit. Arti and Robert followed her lead and slowly made the motions of evacuation. Then they froze. In the deafening silence, they heard footsteps.

The sound was growing louder, almost as loud as the sound of the heartbeats of the three intruders. Whoever or whatever it was, was coming downstairs, coming to the great hall, coming to the three terrified teenagers.

The footsteps simply got louder and faster, until they were booming, and seemed not only to originate from the stairwell, but from the entire building. The three stood frozen, peering into the shadows, desperately trying to see who or what their pursuer was. The

51

booming was so loud now that the windows were rattling. The group headed for the door. Their feelings of panic were overwhelming, and as they reached the door frame, the booming steps reached the bottom of the stairwell in an incredible thud. Arti turned and yelled out, "Hello, who's there?" into the darkness of the great hall. Nothing could have prepared him for his answer. A bone-chilling bloodcurdling demonic scream of a man in anguish, ending in the snarl of some rabid beast, split the air around the three teenagers.

"Get out! Get out! Get out!" Arti screamed. He pushed his pals out the door toward the car, and as he moved to shut the door, he was flung with tremendous force onto the ground outside. He wasted no time in figuring out what had happened. He just ran for the car, slid into the driver's seat, rammed the keys into the ignition, and spun the tires—getting the gang "the heck outta here!"

At a safe distance, which incidentally was through two cities and across the Tennessee River bridge in another county, they came to a stop. All of them were pale, panting, and on the verge of hyperventilating. Arti interrupted the heavy breathing and pounding heartbeats. "Is everyone okay?"

"Arti, what's that on your cheek? There's something red on your face. Turn on the overhead light. Let me take a look at you," said Maggie.

On the right side of Arti's face, a hand print was clearly visible against his once olive, now ghostly white, complexion. They all took turns placing their hands in the reddened impression, only to discover that it was abnormally large.

"Creepy!" Robert shuttered.

"Oh, Arti! It hit you!" Maggie was concerned understandably.

"What was that thing?" stammered Robert. "What in the world was that thing!? What was it!?" he sat in shock still panting.

"I don't know, but I don't think I'm going back there. I've had enough of playing patty cake with demons. How about y'all?" Arti was getting his sense of humor back. The teenagers giggled and boasted about what they would have done if they had gotten the chance. "I'd open up a can of whoop exorcism on his butt if he tried that patty cake stuff with me!" growled Robert as he beat his chest Tarzan style.

"Then I'd give him an offer he couldn't refuse! See you later buddy!" this time in his best Alabama gangster impersonation. They laughed. Maggie said, "I don't know about you guys, but I think that was the most exciting thing that *ever* happened to me! Talk about entertainment! Arti, you sure do know how to pick 'em!"

"Yea, umm, I think maybe abandoned buildings are

gonna be taken off my list of things to do! What do y'all think?"

They all agreed.

A few years later, the abandoned building was renovated and became lovely condos. The three teenagers grew up and went to college and still get together on occasion and ride around remembering the adventures of their youth. One evening, they decided to drive by the Villages just to see what, if anything, had changed. As the three slowly glided past the gleaming renovation, they noticed the structure was dark. "I wonder what else is living there with all those people," Arti considered aloud. As they creeped on into the night, a bright light flickered inside.

The Mysterious Figure

The Mysterious Figure

It was Christmas 1982, and the Lewis family had recently moved into a new house—new for them anyway. Built in the twenties, the house was in one of Anniston's most historic neighborhoods. It was located a few blocks off Noble Street, where, on a clear summer's day, St. Michael's could be seen from an upstairs window.

That particular Christmas morning, the family had gathered together in their living room. The children were excited because they had never had a house of their very own. A new house meant a live seven-foot Christmas tree—not the artificial four-foot one they were used to. They had spent their early childhood years moving from place to place, from apartment to apartment. Not only had they been in Anniston for almost a year, but they had been in this house for most of that year. Christmas was the first major celebration they had commemorated in the house.

They rose early that morning to celebrate the season. Per family tradition, every member of the family had his or her picture taken in front of the Christmas tree. The parents, Charlotte and Donald, were always first, followed by Janie, Jessica, and Jason. Then they would have just the children, just Charlotte with the children, and finally, just Donald with the children. Afterward, they would begin to open presents. As the children began to tear into their packages, Donald would walk around capturing every moment on film.

The excitement of the day eventually wore off, and the children went to bed. The next morning, Donald went out to have the pictures developed. He couldn't wait to see them. "Our first Christmas in our very own house," he thought as he drove to the drug store. He couldn't help but feel proud.

Anxiously awaiting the return of the pictures, Donald promised Charlotte that he wouldn't look at them until he arrived back home. The family was eagerly waiting, ready to pounce on him the moment he opened the door.

As they began flipping through the pictures, they noticed a strange figure in some of them. It looked to be the figure of a woman, but was very white and blurry. On a closer look they noticed not all the pictures contained the image, only a few, and the woman was always next to the youngest child, Jason. Puzzled, they assumed it was simply something odd that had happened while the photos were being developed. Looking back through the negatives, they noticed the weird light was present there as well. Donald decided it was the result of the glow from the Christmas tree lights reflecting off the lens of the camera.

Needless to say, the Lewis family was disappointed that the pictures of their perfect first Christmas were ruined.

A few weeks later, it was time for Jason's seventh birthday. Not wanting to repeat the Christmas picture disaster, Charlotte bought a new camera and decided she would become the photographer. As she walked around the party snapping pictures, she was careful there was no glare to mess with the end result.

The pictures were developed a few days later, but the same apparition was present in those as well. It was clear in the one of Jason blowing out the candles on his cake that the mysterious woman was standing next to him smiling. Charlotte and Donald didn't know what to do. There didn't seem to be a logical explanation for why this figure was appearing in the pictures. Charlotte decided to take it upon herself to find out. She located the Christmas pictures and compared them to those from Jason's birthday.

She began by separating them into two stacks: those with the figure and those without. Charlotte looked for any similarities she could find—where in the house they were taken, how many people were in the picture, who was the subject, or where the figure was located in the picture. She concluded that the figure always seemed to hover around Jason. She was in every picture he was. Is Jason in any of the pictures without the figure? she wondered. As she carefully studied the second pile, she quickly noticed that he was not in any of those. Alarmed, Charlotte decided to do a little more digging. She called the realty office they had used in buying the old house and inquired about its history. They were very vague about its previous owners and did not relate any helpful information. She then contacted her neighbors, hoping they might know a little more. They were of less help than the real estate agents.

Not satisfied with the answers she had received, Charlotte visited the Anniston library archives to search for any weird happenings within the house. "Something happened there, I'm sure, but whatever it was, it sure is being kept a secret," she mumbled.

Unable to recover anything of value, she returned home frustrated. Later that night, Jason woke up screaming. As Charlotte ran toward his room, his door suddenly flew open and slammed shut. Opening the door, she found Jason lying in his bed sweating. He told her that the woman from the pictures had appeared to him. "She just stood there, smiling at me."

"Is that all, honey?"

"No, then she waved, blew me a kiss, and disappeared."

"It'll be okay. She won't bother you anymore."

And she didn't. That was the last time the Lewis family ever saw the woman.

Dorothy

Dorothy

Are you excited about your new school, April?" her
mother asked as they backed out of the driveway.

"Not really."

"I'm sure you will love it. Don't you think it will be
fun to go to the same school your parents attended?"

"Oh sure, it will be a blast."

April's parents grew up in Wetumpka. They met in
junior high and had been together since then. They were
a match made in heaven. April's family had only recently
returned to Wetumpka after spending ten years in
Atlanta, Georgia. April's parents wanted to live closer to
their family. They also didn't want April to attend high
school in Atlanta, and thought that the sooner April
transferred schools, the better.

Thus far the move had been a difficult one for April.
She had only been there about a month and didn't really
know anyone. She was only two years old when they
moved to Atlanta, so she didn't have any childhood
friends to fall back on.

As April's mother drove her to school on the first day,
she told April all about going to school there. All the
dances she attended with April's father, the basketball

games she cheered at, the friends she had had since that time. She told April about how there used to be a swimming pool where the gym is now, the teachers she loved and the teachers she hated, some of whom were still there. She continued to reminisce until they had finally reached the school.

"Have a good day, sweetie!" her mother called out as April slammed the car door.

April took a deep breath. "I can do this," she told herself. "After all, I did live in Atlanta."

She walked into the building, immediately noticing the putrid yellow color of the walls. Looks like the place hasn't been painted since my parents went here, she thought. She made her way around a noisy group of teenagers to the head office. There she received her schedule, locker, and a map of the school. Can this place be any smaller? she wondered after glancing at the drawing of three hallways.

April wandered down the hall to her first class—English. Her nose reacted as she inhaled. The pungent odor of cleaning supplies lingered in the air and didn't help the queasy feeling in her stomach.

When she walked into the classroom, she received strange looks from the other students. She chose a desk near the back of the room. The slim girl sitting beside her said, "Hey, I'm Dorothy. Are you new?"

"Yes, today's my first day."

"What other classes do you have?"

As April read off her class list, Dorothy nodded in agreement. They had every class together and immediately hit it off. The rest of the day progressed slowly. Dorothy was the only person who talked to April all day.

"Just ignore everyone in this school, April. They are all snobs," Dorothy informed her as they walked outside.

"Yeah I'm beginning to realize that."

"Well I have to catch my bus. See you tomorrow!"

April's mother was waiting for her in the parking lot.

"How was your first day, dear? Make any friends?"

"It was fine. I met a girl named Dorothy. We have every class together."

"That's wonderful, honey"

April and her mother drove home in silence.

At dinner that evening, April's mother announced that April had made a friend named Dorothy.

"Good for you. What's her last name? Do we know her parents?" her father questioned.

"Her last name's Atwood."

"Dorothy Atwood," her father repeated, trying to remember why that name sounded familiar.

"Find out her parents' names."

At school the next morning, Dorothy was waiting for April at her locker.

"Hey, while I'm thinking about it, what are your parents' names? Mine think they might know yours."

"Oh, Jim and Alice, but how would they know my parents?"

"They went to school here about a hundred years ago and think the place hasn't changed at all."

The girls continued to bond and made plans for the upcoming weekend.

When April arrived home that evening, she told her parents that Dorothy's parents' names are Jim and Alice.

"Jim and Alice Atwood," her father repeated. April's parents exchanged a weird glance, but neither said anything.

April proceeded to ask if she could stay at Dorothy's the following weekend.

"Sure, honey, as long as we meet her parents first," they responded.

The next day at school Dorothy and April finalized their plans. Friday had arrived before they knew it, and no one else in school had yet spoken a word to April. During gym, one of the other girls asked April about her weekend plans. Startled by the sudden friendliness of a classmate, April replied that she would be staying at her friend Dorothy's.

"Oh, is that a girl from your old school?"

"No, she goes here."

"What grade is she in?"

"Ours. She's in this gym class. She's standing by the water fountain."

They looked to the water fountain, but no one was there.

"What's her name again?"

"Dorothy Atwood," April repeated, exasperated.

"There's no one by that name in our class."

"Yes, there is. I talk to her all day every day. We sit together at lunch."

"No, you sit alone at lunch talking to yourself," another classmate chimed in.

April shot her a nasty look and walked off toward the gym. The other girls followed, whispering, "Dorothy Atwood, isn't that the girl…"

"Ssshhh! You know you're not supposed to say her name out loud."

They hesitantly entered the gym. While playing volleyball, it grew eerily quiet. The faint sound of water splashing caused the girls to stop their game. Suddenly, a voice called out, "Help!"

"That's Dorothy!" April exclaimed.

"Help me!"

April frantically searched the gym, but Dorothy was no where to be found.

"Dorothy, Dorothy! Where are you?"

A gargled reply, "In the pool!" was barely audible over the splashing, which slowly grew fainter, until it stopped.

As April continued to scream and tried to get help, a teacher rushed over to calm her. Mrs. Morris proceeded to tell April the story of a girl named Dorothy who had drowned in the pool in 1976. The girl often befriended new students. Dorothy didn't have many friends, so she always tried to make the new students feel welcome. April was saddened by Dorothy's story and repeated it to her parents after school. They consoled their upset daughter by telling her that they had graduated with Dorothy's older sister, Marie. When April had come home talking about Dorothy, they had a strange feeling it was the same girl. "But we didn't want to frighten you, honey, until we knew for sure."

"Gee, thanks a lot!" April yelled as she ran off to her room.

"She'll be fine. She'll recover."

"I hope you're right."

The next morning April was nervous about school but went anyway. She held her head up high and walked in as if nothing had happened. She sat at her usual table during lunch, and three other girls joined her. No one ever mentioned the Dorothy incident again.

The Old Man at the Lake

The Old Man at the Lake

John and his dad, Mark, were finally on their way to the lake. They had to drive all the way across the state to get there, but the important thing was they were going. They had been planning this trip for months. A whole weekend of camping, fishing, waking up early to catch breakfast, and sitting by the fire all night roasting marshmallows. John was too excited to sit still. He needed this break from work and school. He needed the break from his girlfriend, too. She had been especially annoying that week. Mark was also looking forward to this trip. He hardly saw his son anymore since he started college.

"So how's school, son?" Mark asked.

"Oh, you know," John's usual reply.

"Well, then how's work?"

"The same."

"Aren't we talkative this morning." Mark sighed heavily.

His dad just didn't get that he was tired of talking. Talk, talk, talk. That's all Carmen ever wanted to do—talk. "Hey, Dad, do you think we can just chill this weekend? I really just want to clear my head a little. I'll talk when I'm ready."

"Whatever you say, son."

They continued on in silence.

"So where exactly are we going?"

"Lake Tohlocco."

"Which is where again?"

"Near Ozark."

"Right."

More silence.

"You know your grandfather used to take me here once a year when I was a kid."

Ah, great. Another nostalgia trip, John thought. Just what I needed, a weekend of reminiscing about the old days. He sighed.

John's dad grew up in Ozark. His parents had moved there a few months after Mark was born. The family had a small house just outside of town. Mark's dad made a point to have an annual father-son fishing trip. They took the trip every year until Mark left for college in Tennessee.

Mark had always wanted to do the same with John, but there never seemed to be time. Mark's dad died suddenly from a heart attack the year before. It was only now that Mark had the strength and courage to return to Lake Tohlocco. He knew it would not be the same as when he was a child, but he hoped he and John could reconnect on the trip. John was always so distant, keeping everyone at arm's length.

"Really? Did you guys catch a lot of fish?"

Uncontrollable laughter erupted from his left. "Of course not, your grandfather always forgot his fishing pole."

"How do you go fishing and forget your pole?"

"That's exactly what I used to ask. Turns out he never went for the fishing; he just wanted to spend some quality time with me away from home."

"Oh."

"Don't worry. Our poles are in the back."

"They better be," John mumbled.

"What was that?"

"Oh, okay good."

"Some of the best moments in my life were spent at this lake." Mark continued to talk about his childhood. He told his son about the first fish he caught, the first time he kissed a girl, the first time he watched fireworks over the lake on the Fourth of July. He rambled on about sleeping under the stars and staying up late to watch meteor showers.

John listened as Mark droned on for hours. It wasn't that he didn't like listening to his dad's stories; he just didn't want to hear them for eight hours while stuck in a cramped car. John was ecstatic about finally reaching the lake because it meant an escape from life in the fifties. It also meant an entire weekend in the great outdoors.

The two men quickly unpacked in their rustic cabin.

John's room had a window overlooking the lake. As he gazed out onto the still, lifeless water, he couldn't help but think, This must be what heaven's like. He looked to the left and saw his dad setting up the fire pit. "Guess I could go help him," John said to himself.

"How 'bout hot dogs for dinner?"

"Sounds perfect."

As they munched on their supper, John began to open up to his dad. He talked about school, work, and even got some advice about his relationship with Carmen. After dinner, they did a little night fishing. After several hours of not catching anything, Mark decided to call it quits for the evening, and the guys leaned their poles against the side of the cabin. John stayed up late that night to talk to Carmen. While waiting for the fire to die down, he noticed a man walking around the lake. Glancing at his watch, he saw it was about two o'clock. Just thinking he was seeing things, he turned in.

The next morning John's fishing pole was missing. Unsure of where it could be, he mentioned it to his dad. Both men found it strange that a just a few hours before, both poles were leaning against the cabin and now only one was there.

"Who would steal a fishing pole? And why would you just steal one? If you were going to go to the trouble to take one, why wouldn't you just take both?"

"There are other things to do at a lake than fish, John. Don't get discouraged."

"Oh really, what do you have in mind? Wake boarding?"

"That sounds fun. What is it?"

John laughed hysterically at his father's innocence. "Why don't we just rent jet skis?"

"Your wish is my command."

The father and son spent the rest of the day on Lake Tohlocco trying to throw the other off his jet ski. Exhausted, they headed back to their camp in time for dinner. Opting to once again stay up late talking to his girlfriend, John sat out beneath the stars. He heard the rustle of leaves coming from the lake. Turning towards the calm water, he could barely make out a figure. He strained to see more clearly, only to find the man from the night before—this time with *his* fishing pole. John jogged over to talk to him, but when he was close enough to speak to him, the man disappeared. Okay, now I know I'm seeing things, John thought as he headed back to the cabin.

The next morning, his pole was sitting exactly where he had left it two days earlier. John mentioned the incidents to his dad, but his reply was that John wasn't getting enough sleep. "All this fresh air must be getting to you."

Since John had his pole back, they took off for the bait shop. Making small talk with the owner, Mark casually brought up the incidents with the strange man and the pole. The shop owner described the man perfectly.

"No one really knows who it is, but he is seen quite often. Every six or seven years, someone will lose a fishing pole, only to find it the next day."

"Have these incidents ever been investigated?"

"Oh, no, I don't think so. You boys have a nice day. Come back to see us."

John and Mark left the store, slightly more confused than when they entered. As they paused to hold the door open for another customer, the owner called out, "But you be careful, son. Someone always comes up missing within a few days of seeing the man." The men chuckled as they continued to walk away.

Out on the lake, John and Mark had the perfect fishing day. The weather was just right—not too hot and not too cold. The sun was shining; the sky was clear. Even the fish were behaving. John caught six bass, and Mark caught eight. They celebrated that evening with a fish fry. After dinner they packed up what gear they could in order to leave first thing in the morning. Now his nightly ritual, John stayed up with the fire and Carmen. Hearing something in the bushes, he whipped around to find nothing. "I have lost my mind," he said as he turned back towards the fire. Suddenly everything went black as a rope tightened around his throat.

John sat straight up in bed, his heart pounding and pulse racing. He was sweating profusely. The sun was just beginning to peek through his window when he looked out to see the strange old man walking beside the lake. He continued to stare and watched the gauzy figure slowly fade away into nothingness.

Alabama Tales

Alabama Tales

Catherine slowly opened the heavy doors. She walked inside and sighed, soaking in the moment. She couldn't believe she was here. The Alabama Theatre. She had been dreaming about dancing on this stage for as long as she could remember.

Both Catherine's mother, Diane, and grandmother, Estelle, had spent a lot of time here. Estelle had been in the Miss Alabama pageant several years in a row. Diane had grown up watching movies here and was amazed by the Mighty Wurlizter pipe organ.

Catherine remembered being told of the night her grandmother died. Estelle and her husband had just taken Elizabeth to see a movie. After the show, the family was pulling out onto Third Avenue, when a car came out of nowhere, hitting them head on. Estelle was killed on impact.

A few months after the accident, Diane and her father moved to Richmond, Virginia. He couldn't bear driving by the theatre everyday on his way to the office. Diane never had another opportunity to go to the Alabama. After many years, Diane moved back to Birmingham with her husband and daughter.

Catherine begged her mother to allow her to take ballet. "All my friends take and get to perform at the Alabama Theatre," she would say. "I've heard you talk about the theatre so much, I just have to dance there." After much reluctance, Diane gave in, and Catherine was having her first recital.

Catherine made her way backstage to the dressing rooms. She was in awe of the early twentieth-century architecture of the building. She traced the outline of a door with her fingertips. She knew it wasn't the original gold-leafed door, but using her imagination, she could picture her grandmother walking through the beautiful, shining doors. Her group would perform late in the program, so she and her friends sat around talking.

"There is a lot of history here," she commented to her friend Allie.

"Yeah, there is. Hey, that reminds me. We haven't told any ghost stories yet."

"What do you mean 'yet'?"

"We always tell ghost stories backstage while we await our turn on stage. It's tradition. This is my fifth recital here, and I remember being scared by the older girls during my first one. Now it is my turn to do the scaring."

"What kind of stories do you tell?"

"Oh, you know, the famous ones from those ghost books. The classics every Alabamian knows."

But Catherine didn't know. She listened intently as the other girls chatted.

"This year I have a new one," Allie announced proudly. "This theatre has a ghost."

"Really? Where?" the other girls inquired.

"I'm not sure. I think somewhere upstairs."

"Who is it?"

"My brother said it's a former organ player, coming back to check on things."

"That's creepy."

"What if he shows up while we are on stage? I'll flip out!"

"Brian did say he's been seen in the balcony during performances."

"Okay, now I am scared."

"Relax, you guys," Catherine spoke. "There's no ghost here."

"Okay, so there may not be a ghost here, but there are real ghosts other places." Allie began telling the story of the Red Lady at Huntingdon College in Montgomery.

"A woman known only as the Red Lady can be seen wandering around Pratt Hall," she began. "It all started when a student named Martha moved to Montgomery to fulfill her father's wishes. He wanted her to attend Huntingdon. She became very unhappy shortly after the first month of the semester. She had a hard time making friends, and every time she thought she had, something would happen, causing that girl to leave. And each time she received a new roommate, the new arrangement would only last a few weeks.

"She was finally placed with another roommate and thought this time would be different. But that girl left just like all the others before her. Martha became very depressed and withdrawn."

While she was talking, other girls began to gather around, and some of the younger ones were starting to tremble with fear.

"After no one had seen her all day," Allie continued, "a girl went to Martha's room to check on her. When she opened the door, she found Martha dressed in red from head to toe, lying in a pool of blood. She had bled to death after slitting her wrists. On that very date each year, a girl dressed in all red is seen roaming the halls of the dorm."

When Allie had finished, Ashley related the story of the face in the window of the Pickens County Courthouse.

"In 1878, in Carrollton, Henry Wells was arrested for various crimes and was held in the attic of the Pickens County Courthouse. They kept him in the attic because they were afraid a riot might start since he was accused of burning down the county's previous courthouse two years before.

"Wells was very scared and pressed his face to the window, yelling down to those below that he was innocent. He threatened to haunt the town forever if he was hanged. At that exact moment, lightning struck the building, illuminating Wells's face. Wells was hanged shortly after, and the next morning, his face appeared in the attic window. It's still there today because no one has been successful in removing it."

Rebekah chimed in with one the ghosts of Sloss Furnace. "Legend has it that there are several ghosts haunting Sloss Furnace. I'll only tell you the one about James 'Slag' Wormwood.

"In October 1906, Slag was above the highest blast furnace, known as Big Alice. Somehow he fell into the open pool of liquid iron ore beneath him, instantly melting his body on contact. He wasn't normally up that high on his shift, so its unknown what caused the fall. Some say he became dizzy; others claim he was pushed—no one really liked him much.

"In the years after his tragic death, many workers voiced feelings of uneasiness and 'unnatural presences.' One workman claims he was pushed, but no one was nearby to do it. In 1971, a night watchman came into contact with a 'half man-half demon' who beat him. The man was looked at by a doctor who said he was 'covered with intense burns.'"

Suddenly, a voice called out "Hey!"

The girls screamed.

"Catherine, Allie, Ashley! Your group is up!"

"Coming, Miss Stacy!"

The girls headed up stairs to stretch before they went on. Ashley was shaking.

"What's wrong?" Catherine asked.

"I'm still afraid that organist guy is going to be sitting out there staring at me."

"Just ignore Allie. That was some stupid story her brother told her to scare us. You'll do great tonight."

As the girls finished up their number, there was a flash of light and what appeared to be a strange movement in the back row of the theatre.

"Did y'all see that?" Ashley shrieked after the performance.

"Yeah, I did!" Allie called out shakily.

"See what?" Catherine remarked. "That was just the lights reflecting off the doors."

As the girls peeked out towards the doors, they saw the far left one slowly open and shut, but there was no one near enough to touch it.

"Whatever, Catherine, doors don't just open and close by themselves."

"You just think you are seeing things because you desperately want to see something."

The girls hurried back to the dressing rooms. Having finished their recital, they packed up to leave. Catherine would be meeting her parents in the lobby.

"Bye, you guys!" she called to her friends.

"You guys? This is Alabama, Catherine. We say y'all here."

"Fine, bye y'all," Catherine said in her best Southern accent, trying to keep from laughing. She saw her parents and rushed to meet them.

"You did a wonderful job," her parents congratulated her. "A truly beautiful performance."

"Thanks. Let's go home." The family walked out onto the sidewalk. "Oh wait, I left my jacket backstage."

"Well, go get it. We'll wait here for you."

Catherine made her way back to the dressing room. When she resurfaced in the auditorium, no one else was around. She opened the doors to the lobby and paused, taking in one last look before leaving. Starting out the doors into the lobby, she thought she heard something. She turned around, seeing no one. Suddenly, organ music began to fill the empty auditorium. Looking at the organ, she saw there was no one there to play it.

Frightened, she hurried outside to her parents. Walking down the street to the parking deck, she could still hear the eerie music playing.

The Mystery of Brower Patch Drive

The Mystery of Brower Patch Drive

In a very secluded part of western Blount County, there is a community called Bangor. Best described as detached from civilization, this area lies on the Mulberry Fork of the Black Warrior River.

In a particularly picturesque spot on Brower Patch Drive, there lies an old house on the edge of a bluff. Surrounding the house are hundreds of large loblolly pines, red oaks, and hickory trees.

These trees had been weakened by windstorms and were in danger of being completely destroyed. Before this happened, the property owner wanted to have the trees examined by a forester. An expert on forest management met the man on his property one breezy spring day.

The men began by walking around the property, with the forester examining the trees in the most danger first. He found the land full of red maples, dogwoods, and redbuds. Being spring, the dogwoods and redbuds were in full bloom, adding a level of beauty to the peaceful setting. I would love to have a place like this, the forester thought. He went on to inquire about the history of the property.

The land had been in the man's family for several generations. His father had lived in the house during the

1920s. Then it was primarily used as a summer home and weekend retreat. His father had been a doctor in Birmingham and had allowed some of his patients to use the home.

"Would you like a tour of the house?" the man asked the forester.

As the men walked into the house, a chill ran up the forester's spine. They found the inside unkempt with cobwebs, dust, and mold. It was dark and damp, with a lingering musty, closed-up smell. To the surprise of the forester, several pieces of furniture and other objects remained in the abandoned house. His eyes were drawn to the far corner. There in the darkness stood what appeared to be a beautiful antique piano. The piano looked as though it hadn't been touched in decades.

The forester was drawn to it. He found his legs moving beneath him, edging him closer to it. He reached it, and ran his fingers across the keys. The years of neglect had left inches of dust caked upon them.

The piano was buffet-style with a short keyboard. It was mounted on four huge legs with intricate carvings. The top was open, allowing for a full view of every string and hammer. It had a short keyboard with only seventy-seven keys.

"You have to tell me about this piece," he said. "It's absolutely beautiful. Where did you get it?"

"It has been in my family for many years. It actually dates back to pre-Civil War days. It had been in an old boarding house that belonged to one of my distant relatives. When they sold the boarding house, a music teacher bought the piano. Several years later, my great-grandmother bought it back from the teacher. They eventually moved it here."

"That's amazing," the forester replied, still in awe.

"It actually has had a interesting past here."

The man related the story of the piano as they continued to wander around the house. The forester tried to ignore the creepy feeling of the place as he listened to the man.

"My father had a patient that had been a vaudeville performer. She developed a severe case of tuberculosis, forcing her to leave the stage. She became very depressed, eventually becoming a recluse. Thinking that a little peace and quiet would help her heal, he let her stay here for several months. He thought it would help her stay out of the public eye. Being here alone, she often played the piano, concentrating on some of her old stage songs that had special meaning to her. One in particular, 'I Don't Want to Walk Without You,' touched her because of her relationship with her lover. That's really all I know. I'm not even sure what happened to the woman. My father never explained why she left or where she went."

After a little more exploring, the men left the house and walked across the ancient pool deck area, which was severely overgrown with vines. As they climbed a hill to look at another area of trees, they heard strains of music wafting through the cool morning air.

When the forester heard the music playing, he stopped and whipped around toward the house. The other man said that he had heard the music before. Other people had told him they had heard it as well. "No one has ever had the courage to go back into the house after hearing it," he said.

The forester grew up hearing ghost stories on his grandmother's sleeping porch late at night in a small, rural town, where the only night sounds to be heard were the howling wind, hoot owls, and the occasional wail of a stray tomcat looking for adventure. He was intrigued by the music and the incomplete story of the woman and asked if they could investigate the mysterious music.

As they silently approached the front door, they could see shadows moving inside—three to be exact. The old actress was at the piano, with a couple dancing off to one side embraced in a slow dance. Mesmerized, the forester took in the scene. He turned from the door and looked behind him. The men exchanged glances in disbelief.

Suddenly the music stopped and a shot echoed

throughout the house. Upon turning back to peer into the doorway, the men found there was no one around. Letting his curiosity get the best of him, the forester walked into the parlor area where he had seen the figures. Looking around on the floor, he saw no evidence that anyone had been there. The dust that had built up over the years lay undisturbed. There should be footprints on the floor, the forester thought. The piano was just as he left it, with bat guano, rat droppings, and other disgusting things caked upon it.

Now somewhat nervous and anxiously waiting for something else to happen, the forester took a closer look. In the extremely dim light, he could make out that something was on the keys of the piano, some type of sticky goo or paint. Pulling a small flashlight out of his pocket, he bent down to get a better look. To his amazement and horror, the piano keys were covered in blood.

Whose was it and how did it get there? How long has it been there? Was it there when he ran his fingers across the keys? If so, why didn't he feel the blood then? Had he really witnessed what he thought he had, or had it just been his imagination? If it had happened, who was dead, and who had pulled the trigger? If someone had been shot, where was the body? Was there ever really anyone there in the first place?

These questions and more raced through the forester's mind. Realizing he hadn't heard a peep from the other man, the forester turned around looking for him. He was going to ask the man if he knew anything else about the history of the house, but the man was cowered in the corner shaking.

The forester decided to leave the house for the sake of its owner, but as he drove away he couldn't help but wonder about what had really happened all those years ago on Brower Patch Drive. Who were the woman and the couple he saw dancing? Was the woman a victim or a murderer? Would he ever receive an answer to these questions?

The Cross Garden

The Cross Garden

"William Carlton Rice was a very dedicated man," Amber began a speech for her public speaking class. Her assignment was to relate to the audience an interesting and meaningful life experience—something that had had a profound impact on her. It had been easy for her to pick her topic. A few months earlier she had an eye-opening experience in Prattville.

"He was dedicated to his faith and felt he was called to caution people about hell before they died. His message lives on, even after his own death." She paused to hold up pictures of Rice's famous Cross Garden.

"There are hundreds of wooden crosses on his property. Each holds its own unique message for the viewer. Some of the most notable, and memorable, include "Hell is hot hot hot" and "You will die." Parts of scripture also appear on pieces of old rusty appliances such as washing machines and refrigerators. There are sections of signs warning of the dangers of sex and drugs.

"Rice began his garden after the death of his mother in 1976. There was a cross wreath at her funeral that inspired him to build his garden. He worked on it for almost twenty years, always adding more to the eleven-acre garden. His testament has led many to salvation. He often compared himself to Noah in interviews with various magazines, newspapers, and travel web sites. The garden has also been featured in several folk art books.

"After reading about this man, his faith, and his mission to save the world, I myself traveled down Autauga County Road 86 to view the garden." Amber continued telling her story of seeing the messages and feeling inspired. But she didn't tell the class the whole story.

The previous summer Amber and her boyfriend were driving back to Sylacauga from Montgomery. Derek had read about the Cross Garden in a book about weird places in Alabama. He decided he would try to find it the next time he was in the area. After finding it, he knew Amber would want to see it as well.

One Friday evening it happened to be on their way home. Telling Amber they would take a slight detour that unusually cool August night, Derek made his way onto County Road 86. Suddenly, he stopped in the middle of the road and told Amber to look to the left. Peering through the darkness, she saw hundreds of crosses on the hill next to the road.

Each cross was handcrafted with black hand-lettered words. No two were alike. "Repent. Turn back now. Sex is sin," Amber read. "Gees, those are a little harsh, don't you think?"

"Just wait," Derek stated as he inched a little farther up the road. "Now look to your right."

"Whoa!" Amber nearly jumped out of her seat. Hundreds more were staring at her in the moonlight. The signs on that side of the road were a bit harder to read in the darkness, but it was clear they were warning her about hell. The two simply sat there, soaking in their surroundings. They felt inspired by the faith of whoever fashioned these crosses and signs, but at the same time, they found the warnings brought intense feelings of guilt and fear.

"Hey, what was that?"

"What?"

"I thought I saw something move over there."

"Over where, Derek?"

"Over by that old truck." He pointed to the right.

As Amber looked in that direction, she noticed a large cross mounted to the back of an ancient, rusty pick-up truck. Overwhelmed with anxiety, she started shaking. She could tell there was definitely something moving in the shadows but could not figure out what it was. There appeared to be a pair of beady red eyes glaring at them in the darkness. Then a raccoon darted out from under the truck.

Derek and Amber laughed hysterically at themselves for being worked up over a simple animal.

"Come on, Derek, let's go. This place is spooky."

Derek slid from park into drive and pressed on the gas pedal. But the car didn't budge. He tried it again and again. He even shut off the engine and recranked it. "This has never happened before," he said worriedly. The car still wouldn't move. It was as if something had a hold on it, keeping it from going anywhere.

"What's going on?" Amber asked, frightened.

"I don't know. It just won't go."

Suddenly the car jerked forward, and the couple sped out of sight. Derek's heart was still racing as he stopped at a gas station a few miles away.

"Sorry, I just need a quick break." He got out and walked around the car. There in the moisture on the hood of the car was what appeared to be a giant hand print.

Amber finished her speech and sat down. Her heart raced as she remembered what had really happened that night.

Hanby's Ghost of Pinson

Hanby's Ghost of Pinson

In the early years of Alabama statehood, the Hanby clan was a prominent family. David Hanby would become one of the earliest businessmen of the state. In 1844, he operated a fleet of some twelve barges carrying coal he had mined in Jefferson County's first mining operation. These coal barges were floated to Mobile. Hanby received from $4 to $7 a ton for the valuable product, which he showed the people of Mobile how to burn. The year 1844 was particularly good because he made a $6,000 profit, quite a tidy sum for those times. He used this money to buy a farm in Pinson, hoping to one day expand his business.

When the Civil War rolled around in the 1860s, Hanby was an old man who had in fact broadened his business interest to include grist mills. Being a member of the Home Guard, he supplied the families of fighting soldiers with flour at a reduced rate. Unfortunately, while Pinson area men were fighting for the Confederacy, Union troops, under the command of General John Thomas Croxton, marched through the area on April 19, 1865. They were in route to Montgomery marching along the Narrows Road bordering Turkey Creek in Pinson.

Several of Croxton's soldiers came upon David Hanby as he was frantically searching his two hundred acre farm for some lost cattle. Yelling for Hanby to halt, the soldiers approached. They yelled a second time for him to stop where he was. Hanby, with his back to the soldiers, continued his search. A soldier quickly shot him in the back, thus ending Hanby's life. He had never heard the soldiers command because he had become quite deaf in his old age.

Hanby's body was later found in a wooded area by several family members and neighbors. He was buried in the family burial plot located on the hillside near the Hanby homeplace across from Turkey Creek Falls.

David Hanby's spirit lingers in this area, searching for his lost cattle. It sometimes appears on dark nights where a wagon or, in later years, a car would snake along the winding Narrows Road. Upon reaching the area of Turkey Creek Falls, the lone occupant of a vehicle would hold his breath hoping not to encounter Hanby's ghost.

One such incident happened a few years ago as a high school English teacher made his way home one night after a long day of teaching, grading papers, putting together club newsletters, and those never-ending lesson plans. It was in the early fall, and the school had just held an open house for parents and students to meet with the teachers. After all the questions had been answered and everyone had gone home, it was finally time to call it a day.

As Mr. Davis was cruising toward home along Narrows Road, he thought about the stories he had heard about Hanby's ghost as a child. He wondered if he might ever be privileged to see such a sight himself. He moved along slowly, glancing in the direction of Turkey Creek Falls now and then.

Maybe it was the lateness of the hour after a long and exhausting day, maybe it was the fog that was beginning to roll in, or maybe it was just an overactive imagination, but as he peered out the window toward the Falls, Mr. Davis was startled to see a white image in the distance. He slowed the car even more, scanning the open area just ahead.

A chill ran up his spine and goose bumps broke out all over his arms. His hands were clinched around the steering wheel, his knuckles slowly turning white. Surely, this couldn't actually be Hanby's ghost, he thought. I must be seeing things.

He closed his eyes, hoping to clear his vision. Opening them, he peered into the distance, squinting. What shape would it take? Where would it go? His mind was racing with ideas, but he couldn't decide what to do next.

Like most of the faint-hearted, he froze. Stopping the car, he just sat there staring out the window. He wanted to get out, but he couldn't move his legs. After what seemed like an eternity of watching this strange white shape moving all around the field, he managed to open the car door. He moved slowly, easing himself out of the car. He put two feet on the ground and found that his legs were shaking so he could hardly stand.

"One step at a time," he said aloud. "Just put one foot in front of the other. You don't want to miss this." He walked along toward the ghostly figure but was afraid to breathe. He didn't want to scare it away, whatever "it" was.

Wait, what was that sound? He panicked. Could it be a voice calling for cattle? Surely that was the sound he heard. Then whoosh! A little sports car roared by at a fast speed. Of course, pure reflex caused Mr. Davis to turn and look at the car speeding by. Alas, when he turned back around, he couldn't find the figure again. The shape was gone. He had missed his chance to meet with the famous Hanby ghost.

The Lovers of Big Bridge

The Lovers of Big Bridge

There is a bridge in Cullman County that everyone calls Big Bridge. Today it spans a narrow channel of Lewis Smith Lake, but before the Warrior River was damned by Alabama Power Company in the late fifties and early sixties, there was a deep chasm there, with sandstone cliffs that dropped sharply to a bottom far below—one that couldn't even be seen through the clotted trunks of beeches and pines that clung to the rocky walls.

The real name of the bridge is Phillips Bridge, but no one ever calls it that. No one ever did. It was a favorite haunt of kids out for a joyride, lovers out for a tryst, and those just up to no good. You could throw just about anything off the side of that bridge and never hear from it or see it again. There are lots of stories about the bootleggers up in that dry part of the state, who tossed their illegal cargo over the bridge to evade capture by the revenuer men. Of mountain men who hid down there to avoid conscription by either side during the Civil War. And of deep dark nights when those who crossed the wrong men at the wrong time in the wrong place were forcibly separated from this life and ejected off the bridge into the abyss below.

Then the power company built the Lewis Smith dam downstream, the deep gullies and canyons filled up with water, and who and what had gone over the side of Big Bridge stayed down there, their secrets safe forever.

If there were no such thing as ghosts, maybe none of those secrets would ever have come to see the light of day, or the moonlight of night, again. But when the moon is waxing, there are those who say there are wraiths misting up out of the waters of the lake, drifting across the bridge, hovering as if in wait for something.

There is a theory about these wraiths. Some say it is true, some say it is nonsense. But the reality no doubt lies somewhere in between.

It was 1939—the outbreak of World War II. Hitler was invading Poland when Betsy Daniels met Joshua Brown at a church supper in Crane Hill. Joshua was new to the area. His parents had relocated to the Bremen area, just a few miles down the road from Betsy's parents' chicken farm. Josh's father had lost his job in Pittsburgh, and the family had relatives in Alabama. With Josh's mother ill and nowhere else to go, they had moved in with them. At eighteen, Josh was tall and strong, with raven dark hair, dark skin, and arresting eyes: one was blue and the other green. He got his coloring from his mother, who was Greek, and his unusual eyes from his father's Irish side of the family.

Betsy couldn't take her eyes off him at the church supper. There was singing followed by a covered dish picnic on the grounds of the little church near the settlement of Trade. Betsy's aunt and uncle owned the general store there in Trade, and proudly supplied many of the treats offered up on this special day— Homecoming—at the church. After Betsy's father had said the Lord's Prayer, everyone went out to the grounds to dig into the wonderful spread that lay before them, in the shade of the trees.

Betsy's mother noticed her petite blond daughter staring at Joshua and cautioned her to stay away from the unknown young man. "You don't know anything about him," she scolded. "He's too old for you, and he's from up north somewhere. Just let him be." She yanked Betsy's arm and drew her away to visit with some relatives on the other side of the crowd.

But the die was cast. Betsy and Joshua were bound to run into each other again, and they did, not more than a week later at her aunt and uncle's store. Josh smiled at her and asked if he could help her carry anything home. She told him her mother would never allow it, but lingered for a moment to learn his name.

Their flirtation escalated with the war. About a year after their first meeting at the store, Joshua and his father were walking down the road past Besty's farm, on their way to help build a barn, and stopped to see why Betsy was crying under a tree. Her kitten, Maggie, had climbed to the top of the tree and wouldn't come down. Betsy's father didn't like animals much and had forbidden Betsy to climb the tree after the little cat—had even promised he would shoot it out of the tree if it didn't come down on its own. Betsy was beside herself with despair and worry.

Joshua told her not to fret. He dropped his rucksack and immediately started up the tree. Within five minutes he had the kitten back in her hands. Betsy was overjoyed and wanted to do something for Josh in return. She stooped and picked up a blue jay feather and gave it to him as a memento. Josh smiled and pocketed the feather. "I'll keep it next to my heart," he promised.

And then he whispered, "I'm going to marry you someday."

Their fate was sealed.

Betsy began to make a lot more trips to the general store than were needed. At the hint that anything was needed at home, up she would jump and run. Josh did the same, and the next time they encountered each other, he pressed a note into her hand. "Can you meet me tonight at Big Bridge?" it read. Betsy nodded silently.

And so began their trysting. Under the moonlight, under the stars, in all but the very worst kind of weather, the sweethearts crept away from home at night and met on the bridge. There wasn't much traffic in those days, and they would sit and dangle their feet and talk about their dreams, or creep under a tree and gaze down into the dark chasm and kiss and make their plans.

Until one night. Josh was late. Betsy didn't think he was going to show up at all. She had almost begun to doubt him, to wonder if he had found another girl, been caught by his parents, or injured. Her thoughts raced. Then she heard his footstep. His face was dark and somber; even in the moonlight she could tell something was wrong.

"I'm going overseas," he told her. "To help Uncle Sam win this war. I head out in the morning."

Betsy broke down. She couldn't bear to let go of the love of her life. Josh calmed her. "It's all right. I'll come back to you, I promise. We'll be married as soon as the war is over."

His blue and green eyes fixed on her. He took the blue jay feather out of his pocket and handed it to her. "Keep this close to your heart until then," he said.

Betsy went about her life as best she could after that. The war had reached the little farming community and everything was rationed. Money was short and the days were long. She helped with the chickens, milked the cow, and rolled out biscuits and pie crusts for her mother. From time to time she slipped away at midnight to Big Bridge and sat looking at the moon and the stars and wondering if, half way across the world, Joshua was looking at the same moon and stars. Somehow the days, then the years, passed. Occasionally Josh's younger sister, Juliet, would bring her a note or word of Josh. He was all right. He'd made it through several battles safely.

She kept everything from him, every scrap of paper, along with the blue jay feather, in a box in a hollow tree near the bridge.

And then came the telegram. Juliet walked all the way up to the Daniels farm one day, her eyes rimmed with red. Betsy saw her outside the kitchen window and knew. He was gone. Lost at Normandy.

Betsy felt strangely calm. That night as she climbed into bed, she still had her clothes on under her nightgown. She knew what she must do.

At midnight she drifted down the road to Big Bridge, as if she were a ghost already. She sat by the hollow tree, reading his letters one last time. Then she tucked the beloved blue jay feather into her bodice, next to her heart. She walked calmly to the middle of the bridge, paused to say a prayer, and stepped off into the deep, deep darkness to join Joshua in eternity.

Her body was never found.

Joshua would know, because he spent weeks looking

for her when he returned from the war. The telegram had been a mistake. A case of mistaken identity. He'd come home, all the long and dusty miles, to find his Betsy had gone to meet him elsewhere. He felt he owed it to her to put her at rest. But he couldn't find her. At least, not anywhere in the bottomless chasm below Big Bridge. There was only one place he could go now to find his Betsy. So that is where he went.

Just as she had, Joshua chose a midnight when the stars were bright and high light clouds sailed past the moon, throwing just enough shadows on the ground to make you wonder where your next footstep might lead. Just like Betsy's, Josh's feet found the place where he would be together with his true love forever.

The lake's waters have covered the lovers now for the rest of time.

But on a moonshadowed night, when your eyes seem to be playing tricks on you, folks say you can see the shapes of two lovers yearning toward each other on that bridge. And if you drive past late at night and your headlights catch a glint of blue and a glint of green for a fraction of a second, it just might be Joshua and his lost love. There are some things that last forever, even if they can't be fully explained.

Troop

Troop

In the last sixty years or so, a few strange things have been reported around Tuscumbia. People have been helped, or guided, or even rescued by an unexplained presence.

Back in the 1940s an airman was home on leave from the war. He'd borrowed his parents car to go see his girlfriend, who lived over toward Barton on the Tennessee River. It was an old car and not in good running condition, but the airman, whose name was Bud, was so excited about seeing his girl that he didn't give a thought to anything else. He set off after supper with his thoughts all on her.

It was late in the year and night fell quickly. Bud hadn't been on the road too long before the old Ford sputtered and rolled to a stop. He banged his fist on the steering wheel in frustration. Then he banged it again when he saw it wasn't the car's fault; it was his. The car had simply run out of gas.

Bud set off walking. He thought he knew a shortcut that would take him out in his girlfriend's father's east pasture. He'd taken it before and was pretty sure he could find it again, even in the dark. So great was his

desire to see his love before he went back to the front
lines that he struck off down the road. After about a
quarter of a mile, he set off through some scrub that lead
into the woods. He'd been trudging for about an hour
when he realized he had no idea where he was. He
couldn't even tell if he was going in a straight line or in a
circle. Bud realized he had made a mistake, and for the
first time in a long time, he was a little scared. He
stopped under a big pine and tried to pull his thoughts
together, saying a prayer.

It was then he heard the baying of a hound. Or was it
just the wind? It stopped. Bud turned around. No, there
it was again, coming from the other direction. He took a
few steps, heard the baying again. He began to walk
toward it. If someone had a hound, that someone could
help him. He continued to walk toward the baying,
which grew increasingly more insistent. Sometimes it
would pause, but always started up again. It got louder
as he walked, sometimes leading him in one direction,
sometimes another. Bud just kept going in the direction
of the hound.

He finally emerged into the pasture he was looking
for. There, a couple of hundred yards ahead, was his
girlfriend's parents' house. The lights in the windows
were the most inviting thing he'd ever seen in his life. He
ran across the pasture.

Funny thing was, when he told his girlfriend and her folks about how their hound led him through the woods, they didn't know what he was talking about. They didn't have a hound, only a few barn cats.

In the early seventies a couple of college kids, home for the summer, were out having a little too much fun one night. Larry and Carol hadn't been that friendly in high school, but that summer after their freshman year at the University of North Alabama in Florence, they suddenly clicked. They both lived in Muscle Shoals, and started hanging out regularly together. Mostly they went to parties at friends' houses, when the friends' parents weren't home. That way they could partake of adult libations without the inconvenient interruption of the adults.

The two teenagers had been out late that summer night at a party near Tuscumbia. Just west of Tuscumbia, in fact. They'd had a little too much to drink but, since there were no adults around to tell them not to drink and drive, and the rest of their friends were in the same condition, no one tried to prevent them from getting in Carol's car and heading back to the Shoals.

It was so late there were few other vehicles on the dark country roads. Larry, who was driving, complicated matters by leaning over to show Carol his affection every few minutes or so. She returned the favor. At a bend in the road it looked like they were headed for serious trouble when the car started going straight instead of following the curve in the road. That was when Carol sat up and shrieked, "You're going to hit that dog!"

Larry, startled out of his amorous, beer-fueled haze, grabbed the wheel and yanked the car back on the road, the tires skidding on the gravelly shoulder, Carol screaming.

Both kids were shaken wide-awake, sobered by the experience. Once back on the road, Carol turned around to see if the dog was all right, but it was gone. It had looked like an old hound dog.

Sue lived in Florence in 1989. She was an elementary school teacher. Her husband had left her the previous year, taking every penny of their savings with him. But Sue was resilient; she'd always been a survivor. She'd made it through the untimely deaths of both her parents and she had vowed she'd make it through this.

She was a waitress on weekends, and after school during the week she made extra money tutoring students of all ages in their homes. It was exhausting work. For the most part, the students were not interested in learning; that was the hardest part. She had to find a way to motivate them—and their parents—before she could begin to help them catch up on their schoolwork. Some of the parents were worse than the kids.

But she'd had her successes, and she was proud of that. After the lessons were finished, she often spent an hour or so having coffee with the parents, discussing this and that. She was usually ready to just run out the door and race back to her little apartment and cat in Florence for a few minutes of peace before bed, but she couldn't very well turn down a family's hospitality.

There was one such occasion that Sue remembered particularly well. It was late one night just before Labor Day. School had started back up and she had been working hard with her students to help them get a jump start so they wouldn't fall behind and get into trouble with their grades again. One especially difficult student named Charlie had kept her late that night. Already he was having trouble with math, and his parents delayed Sue with their questions. Finally everyone settled down for a piece of cake. She couldn't very well refuse that, could she?

It was after ten o'clock when she left for home. The road was dark, there was no moon. Sue was so tired she couldn't keep her eyes open. She turned the radio up loud, but still found herself drifting off. She reached into her purse for a pack of gum and popped a piece into her mouth. Usually the headlights of oncoming cars annoyed her because her vision at night was not good. But she'd give anything this night to see another car, or anything that would keep her awake. The radio faded, went to static, then faded in and out again. She found herself singing to keep her eyes open. In spite of her best efforts, her heavy eyelids dropped and she dozed off.

The only way Sue could explain what happened next was to say it was a dream. She dreamed there was a dog in the car with her on the front seat. It was a loyal old hound dog, red in color with maybe something else mixed in. It didn't make sense that she could see it, with its velvety brown, droopy friendly eyes, and its reddish coat, because she was asleep, wasn't she? But she could see it as the dog shoved its wet black nose up into her ear and snuffled, then licked the side of her face.

She woke up and drove safely, but as fast as she could, back to Florence, where she practically ran from the car into her apartment, and closed and locked the door.

Maybe it's just coincidence, but on Labor Day in 1937, a man named Key Underwood buried his beloved coon dog Troop at his hunting camp about seven miles west of Tuscumbia.

Troop had been his master's faithful companion, hunting with him for more than fifteen years. Troop and

119

Key were inseparable. Troop was part redbone coonhound and part bird dog. Everyone around the tri-cities area knew him. There wasn't a dog born who could measure up to Troop. He was what they call "cold nosed," which meant that he could pick up the coldest coon track there was and follow it until it grew warm and fresh. He never lost a track, and he never lost a coon in his entire life. He never gave up or left the trail until he had that coon treed.

Key Underwood and his hunting friends had many good times telling stories about their dogs, sitting around the camp fire and planning their next hunt. That's why Key chose that special spot to bury his life's companion. It was the spot Troop loved best. Key put Troop in a cotton pick sack and said a prayer over his pal, then marked the spot with a rock from an old chimney. Since that Labor Day in 1937, many hunters have buried their best-loved companions there by Troop. Folks might argue over who had the best coon dog in Alabama, but there is a strong argument that there never has been, and never will be, a dog that measures up to Troop.

The Tannehill Ghost

The Tannehill Ghost

Have you ever visited the ruins of the Tannehill Ironworks? Especially in the fall, winter, or early spring of the year, when few people are around, there is an eerie quality to this secluded historic spot. Tucked into the woods on the banks of the Roupes Creek near McCalla, you can reach it only by footpath. As you get closer to the old works, the atmosphere becomes more and more hushed. You find your voice dropping to a whisper, and then silencing altogether.

There is definitely something haunted about this spot.

And when you come to the end of the path and see the old sandstone walls of the ironworks hulking in the trees, speckled with light and shadow, they seem to tell a story. There seem to be hundreds of voices silenced within those walls, waiting to have their stories told. There is a whisper of more than one presence that has left this earth, but might not have left entirely. You might even feel it, like a breath on your cheek as you stand there.

There are folks who say one of those presences is Jebediah Washington. Jebediah was a slave who worked

122

at the Tannehill furnaces. He lived in a cabin near the ironworks with his brother, Ezekiel, and they were the two hardest workers on the premises. They had been there since 1859, cutting sandstone rocks, hauling them on skids, and stacking them to form the three big furnaces.

The site was named for Ninian Tannehill, who took on the original bloomery forge on the banks of Roupes Creek after its builder, a furnaceman from Pennsylvania named Daniel Hillman, died around 1832. Tannehill thought the forge left behind by Hillman would make a nice addition to his farming business.

The work on the ironworks, which would become key to the Confederate war manufacturing industry, began in earnest in 1859, with the laying of the sandstone block for Tannehill No. 1. Its designer was Moses Stroup, a famous Southern ironmaster. In 1862, a man named William L. Sanders bought the Tannehill furnaces and began expanding the ironworks in earnest, adding outbuildings and support operations.

Tannehill was run as a plantation with as many as six hundred slaves doing the work of hauling the sandstone. The enormous blast furnaces were fired by charcoal, and to make it you had to have trees—a continual, monumental supply of felled trees from the surrounding hills. The operation went at top momentum day and night. Trees were turned into charcoal and used to fuel the hot, hungry mouths of the blast furnaces. A gigantic steam engine kept the blowing machines heating the fires that would melt iron ore. The ore was poured out of a huge bucket into molds shaped like "pigs." Once formed, the pigs were made into all the iron supplies needed in vast amounts by the Confederacy: ordnance, pots, pans, and ovens to support the army. At its peak, Tannehill produced up to twenty-two tons of iron every day.

Jebediah and Ezekiel were part of it. It was hard work, but they had known no other life. They both loved being out in the woods—the smell of the crackling leaves, and song of birds, the satisfaction of sweating your way through a big tree and stepping back, knowing it was about to go. They worked together, each on one end of the big cross-cut saw. That was the best part. They were together. And they had plans. After the war they planned to buy their way to freedom.

They didn't know where the rest of their brothers and sisters were, or their parents. They'd been scattered by the war, spread around to different states. One brother, Jacob, had gone to New Orleans and lived as a free man of color. They'd gotten word from him one time, through their mother, when they were still on the plantation in Georgia. He'd married an octoroon and had a baby on the way.

A second brother had made a run for freedom up north, but they didn't know where he was, or if he had made it or not.

Jeb and Zeke figured they were doing all right for now to have a place to lay their heads, and the opportunity to work together. At night when the work was done, it was mesmerizing to stand and watch the molten iron, glowing like liquid gold, pour out of the ladle into the pigs, and to see the sudden flare of colored light as the slag was poured off. The faces of the working men then, both black and white, were lit with the same light and it was almost possible to imagine them as brothers united in their mission. Then Jeb and Zeke would go back to their cabin and lay on their pallets, and know they had each other. That, and the highly illegal letter from their mother Jeb kept hidden in his shirt next to his heart. He couldn't read, but he knew what it said: "Take care of your brother, and always remember I love you. Go with God. Mama." He repeated the words silently to himself every night before he fell asleep.

And then came the end of the world. It was March 31, 1865. Jeb and Zeke were out in the woods. They didn't know that three companies of the Eighth Iowa Cavalry were pushing through, bearing down upon them in Union General James H. Wilson's campaign to destroy war industry sites in Alabama.

Jeb and Zeke only found out when they heard the commotion, the shots, the cries, and the shrieks of terrified men and horses. They smelled the smoke then, the burning. Their attention distracted, neither man noticed that the tree they'd been cutting was about to fall. Before they could clear away in time, it came down. Jeb thought at first they were clear, but then realized from the fear on his brother's face that there was trouble. Zeke's leg was partially caught under the trunk of the tree.

"Can you move it?" Jeb asked.

Zeke silently shook his head, beads of sweat standing out on his brow. "You run Jeb. You got to run for it."

Jeb stood his ground. "I ain't goin' nowhere without you, Zeke."

He began to push and heave at the trunk of the tree, the commotion of the attack and pungent sting of the smoke growing stronger. "They must've set the whole place on fire," he said.

Zeke urged his brother to leave him. "Mama would want one of us to be saved," he insisted. "You go now. Go!"

But Jeb was stubborn. "I got to get you out from under this tree!"

"Even if you do, I can't walk, Jeb."

"I'll carry you."

126

Jeb shook his head stubbornly and went to find the saw. That was when he came face to face with a Union soldier. He was just thinking it must be a Union soldier, because he was wearing a blue coat, when the soldier shot him dead.

After he killed Jeb, the soldier pushed on through the woods, looking for anyone else who had escaped the destruction. He didn't see Zeke lying under the tree, who eventually died of exposure and blood loss, with his brother, Jeb, lying just a few feet away.

At the end of that terrible day, everything but a few sections of sandstone foundry wall had been destroyed. The tannery, the gristmill, the warehouse, and the cabins where five hundred of the slaves lived were all gone. And so were the dreams of Jeb and Zeke Washington.

But the ghost of Jebediah remains. He can't leave this earth because he promised his brother Zeke he wouldn't go anywhere without him. On certain afternoons and early evenings, when there's no one around, you might sense his presence filtering past your ear or your cheek, maybe ruffling your hair, as he returns in search of Ezekiel, in search of his brother and that freedom they dreamed of together.

Patty's Story

Patty's Story

A woman named Patty cleaned large office buildings in the Birmingham area for a living. It was Saturday evening, so she was at the Sears Home Improvement building located in the Riverchase area just off Valleydale Road. Sears was one of her regular accounts. She always tried to stick to a cleaning schedule: buildings were cleaned at specific times on the same day every week.

Patty usually worked alone, so she figured a regular pattern would keep her aware of what was around her. It wasn't that she was afraid to be alone in the empty buildings, she just liked to be sure she was safe.

This building was one of the most familiar to her; after all, she had been cleaning it for several years. She knew where everything belonged and exactly how long it would take to clean. This particular Saturday should have been no different.

When she walked in, she thought everything to be the same. The floors were dirty as usual, blanketed by cement dust tracked in from outside. The desks were piled up with paperwork. The computers were turned off. Their monitors and green power lights were as black as the night sky.

As she cleaned, she became very hot. The air

conditioner was turned off, and with all the doors shut, there was no air circulating. She paused to catch her breath, wiping the sweat from her forehead. Despite that, a breath of cold air brushed across her face and chills ran up her spine.

She was dumbfounded but continued working. Suddenly, she wasn't alone. She heard voices. "There can't be anyone here but me," she thought. She shut off her vacuum cleaner and paused to listen. There were definitely voices, specifically a man's voice, coming from the corner office. The radio was on. A car commercial was playing. "I wonder why I didn't hear that before," she asked herself.

Just as suddenly as it had begun, the yakking of he car salesman stopped. The radio had shut itself off. Patty simply ignored it and continued her cleaning. She had soon finished. She packed up her things and turned toward the door. She dropped the bottle of cleaner she held in her hand as the color drained from her face. Her eyes grew wide as she stared at a wispy white face in the doorway. She couldn't tell if it was male or female. The moment she blinked, it disappeared.

"Weird night tonight," she thought as she locked up the building to leave and headed out to the car.

She returned home to her family a little shaken but didn't mention the occurrence to anyone.

A hard worker, Patty was given several more large accounts the next week. She also received permission to hire additional help. That Saturday when she returned to the Sears building, she was accompanied by a woman named Jenny. Patty immediately locked the door behind her and checked the other exits and windows. "No one's going to sneak in here tonight and scare me," she thought aloud. She glanced at the clock on the wall. It said 5:30 pm. "Perfect, plenty of time to finish here and clean the BellSouth building before dinner."

This weekend Patty paid more attention to her surroundings. She immediately noticed that it was quiet. She listened as the sound of Jenny's broom sweeping the grime off the floor softly echoed throughout the expansive room. Patty cautiously entered the small corner office that the week before was home to a radio with the life of its own. The radio was off; she double and triple checked to make sure.

"Ah, peace and quiet tonight." She breathed a sigh of relief. Tonight, there was only silence.

The two women were finished cleaning very quickly and packed up to leave. "I guess I was anxious about nothing. It was just my imagination," Patty thought as she loaded the industrial vacuum into the trunk of her car.

"Patty, I left a bottle of Windex on one of the desks. I better go get it," the other woman called out. She emerged from the building a few minutes later with a frightened look on her face.

"What's wrong? Did you even go in? I didn't see the lights come on."

"I didn't have to turn them on," the woman answered. "The whole place was lit up by the computer screens."

"The computer screens? But they were all turned off!"

"I know! But every monitor was on, and let me just say, those people have some interesting pictures on their desktops!"

The women laughed nervously, hoping to forget the incident.

"How did they get turned on?"

"I have no idea, but it was all of them. Not a one was off!"

Confused, Patty knew the woman would be too shaken to help her clean the other building. "Well, thanks for your help, Jenny! See you next week!"

The following Wednesday, Patty stopped by Sears to speak to the receptionist, Gladys. She told her about what had happened the past two Saturdays and asked her if she or anyone else had ever witnessed anything odd. Gladys responded that she personally had not seen nor heard anything but would ask around to find out if anyone else had.

That Saturday there was a note from Gladys taped to the door. It simply said that no one had any knowledge of any strange occurrences. "That figures," Patty mumbled, crumpling the note. "Now they all think I'm crazy."

Jenny had returned to help with a determined look on her face. She seemed to be sending whatever it was that occupied the building a don't-mess-with-me message.

Patty's two daughters had come along to help as well. Ages eight and ten, the girls couldn't help much, but they kept each other company as they dusted. They finished their chore and sat at an empty desk coloring. When the younger suddenly called out, "Mommy, Mommy! Someone's talking to us!" Patty immediately stopped what she was doing and ran over to them.

"What are you talking about?"

"We heard a man talking to us!" the older girl chimed in.

"What did he say?"

"I couldn't understand him."

"Me neither."

The lights began to flicker, went out, came back on, and began to flash again. The radio sprang to life. The exact same commercial Patty had heard weeks earlier resonated throughout the office. Papers began to fly off a shelf on the far wall. Then it all stopped. The chaos ended. The room was still, swallowed in silence. The light calmed itself.

Thankfully, the women were almost finished cleaning. They scurried out the door the second they had completed the last office. Once outside, Patty glanced back and saw two faces staring out at them from a window. She hurried her daughters into her car and sped off quickly.

"That place has to be haunted," Patty later told her husband. She relayed every odd thing that had happened to her over the past three weeks.

"Maybe it was built over an ancient Indian burial ground or something," was the only explanation he could offer.

A few days later Patty ventured down to talk to an office manager. "Surely he knows something," she rationed. But she received the same answer as before. No one knew anything, nor had they themselves witnessed any type of weird occurrence, such as those she mentioned.

Patty continued to have supernatural experiences almost every time she cleaned the Sears building, and to this day, who or what appears to her remains a mystery.

The Ghost of the Flora-Bama

The Ghost of the Flora-Bama

It's a funny thing to think about, a ghost tossing a mullet. But people have seen it. Even after Hurricane Ivan took the good old Flora-Bama away (temporarily, of course), there were people who say that Orville Stickenbacker was still out there on the beach in the moonlight, tossing.

That last full weekend in April is a big day at the Flora-Bama. As anyone can tell you, folks come from miles, even hundreds of miles, around to throw a mullet as far as they can from Alabama across the state line into Florida. And what a party.

Orville Stickenbacker was born and raised in Orange Beach. Even when both of his parents passed away, he didn't know where else to go, so he just stayed. He was a homely boy, with a big nose and receding hairline by the time he was fourteen. He wore glasses with lenses as thick as Coke bottles and still couldn't see. His mother made him wear a bow tie to school every day, and as you can imagine, his life on the playground was a living nightmare. Kids liked to throw sand crabs on him yelling "Stick to Stickenbacker!" and other things that can't be repeated here. Orville just went plodding along.

138

He got a job working at Alvin's Island, a tropical department store in Gulf Shores. He liked it there. People who came in to shop always seemed happy. He was happy to help them find the perfect airbrushed t-shirt or hermit crab or toe ring. Nobody needed anything at Alvin's, not really, unless you count the things that make you happy as things you need. Orville was proud of the fact that he knew how to count change and didn't need the register to tell him how much to give the customer back.

To amuse himself, Orville took to wearing tropical shirts and brightly colored Bermuda shorts even when he wasn't at work. He thought that was pretty kicky. He bought his own hermit crab and named her Jezebel. That seemed pretty daring too. He was really living now.

For the final touch, when he turned twenty-one, he went to the Flora-Bama just to say he had been there. He didn't drink and didn't want to. Orville didn't like the way people acted when they had been drinking. It alarmed him, to say the least. But he did like happy people and there were lots of them at the Flora-Bama, especially outside on the back deck. If you've ever been to the Flora-Bama, you wouldn't have remembered, or even noticed, Orville. He was the kind of person who blended into the wall paneling, no matter how loud his clothes were. You would have walked right by him as if he were invisible, because he was. As if he were already a ghost.

That first time Orville sat on the back deck of the Flora-Bama, on his twenty-first birthday, drinking a Diet Coke, was when he saw his first mullet toss. He was amazed. He had no idea people thought up things like that, let alone did them. It seized his imagination to such an extent that his heart began pounding wildly. He tried to imagine what it would be like, entering the contest...everyone watching...entering that ten-foot-wide circle...tossing that mullet as hard as you could across the state line. Some people didn't throw very far, especially the women and the kids. But some did—well over one hundred feet. The crowd went wild for every contestant; it was as if they were watching the Olympics!

Orville saw himself walking up and taking his place, the crowd hushed, then erupting in cheers as his mullet flew into Florida, beating the world record! Trumpets would blare and drums would sound! He would have his picture in the newspaper!

That would never happen, but it was fun imagining.

Every year after that, Orville made sure to attend the mullet toss. He thought about it all year: what he would wear, what the weather would be like, whether last year's finalists would return. He even enjoyed staying after the event to watch the Flora-Bama staff feed the fish to the birds. It was like Orville was really living a whole lifetime in one day, sitting there with all the happy families and visiting tourists at the Flora-Bama, soaking up the joy into himself, taking away the experience as his birthday present that would last for the whole next year. Then it would be time to come again, that last full weekend in April, always right around his birthday.

Then came the year when Orville knew he wouldn't have another birthday. He had felt the lump when he was taking a shower, and now there were several of them. He began to lose weight, and lacked energy. People at Alvin's began to ask him if he were all right. He'd developed dark circles under his eyes, his skin was pasty, and he got sick a lot, catching every little bug that came along.

Finally his boss at Alvin's asked him if he would like to take a little leave of absence. Orville said, "No, thank you." Then his boss told him he *had* to take some time off. Had he been to a doctor lately? His boss kindly asked if he wanted him to take him to one. Orville shook his head, holding back the tears. He begged the manager to just let him take a long weekend, said he was overtired, needed a little rest that's all.

The manager reluctantly agreed, and looked worried.

After the long weekend Orville didn't feel any better but he came back to work and pretended. He even resorted to applying a little concealer under his eyes, and some of his mother's old blush to his cheeks. Two days later, he told his boss he was going to lunch, and he went home to take a nap. When he woke up it was dark out; more than thirty-six hours had gone by. His boss called the next morning and gently fired him.

Orville still didn't go see a doctor. He knew what he had to do. And it was just a few weeks away.

When the weekend of the toss came he was on the back deck. He had on his best tropical shirt, Jezebel in his pocket. He watched every contestant, thinking at one point he might faint in the hot sun. But fortunately he had his pith helmet with him. When the winner was announced, he stood up and cheered, his voice as loud as it had ever been in his whole entire life.

And then, in the bravest thing he would ever do in his life, after the contest was over, he walked up to one of the Flora-Bama staffers and asked if he might toss a fish, just for the fun of it. The guy gave him a big fish and showed him how to throw it, spinning around and holding it by the tail.

Orville gave it his all. The silver fish sailed through the air, catching and flashing the platinum and gold rays of the early evening light. It was a beautiful thing. It didn't beat the world record. But it wasn't the worst throw of the day either. The guy who worked at the

Flora-Bama even clapped for him. A couple of other people who saw Orville throw smiled, and one girl called out, "Way to go!"

Orville sat on the back deck of the Flora-Bama that night until the last customer left and they closed down the place. The moon came up and the stars came out. They were so moist and close in the velvety night sky that Orville felt he could almost touch them, almost breathe them in.

And then, by himself with his best memory made, he slowly walked across the beach and into the waves.

About the Author

Holly Smith was born and grew up in Alabama, where she learned the stories presented in *Alabama Ghosts*. She holds a B.A. in English from Jacksonville State University, and lives in Birmingham, Alabama, where she works for Crane Hill Publishers.